PRAISE FOR THE ONE-PAGE CONTENT MARKETING BLUEPRINT

"One page of gold! This book offers a simple and valuable one-page blueprint that essentially guides you on how to create a targeted content marketing strategy to achieve long-term success."

— **MARTIN LINDSTROM**, NEW YORK TIMES BEST-SELLING AUTHOR OF *BUYOLOGY* AND TIME MAGAZINE INFLUENTIAL 100 HONOREE

"A well-crafted, well-researched, and insightful book. Content Marketing is challenging, this book equips you with the right tools to drive success."

— **JONAH BERGER**, NEW YORK TIMES BEST-SELLING AUTHOR OF *CONTAGIOUS* AND *THE CATALYST*

"Content marketing is not easy...but it's mandatory for innovative and growing companies. The One-Page Content Marketing Blueprint simplifies a complex process so that any company, of any size, in any industry can develop an action-oriented plan that delivers results."

— **JOE PULIZZI**, FOUNDER OF CONTENT MARKETING INSTITUTE AND BEST-SELLING AUTHOR OF *EPIC CONTENT MARKETING* AND *THE WILL TO DIE*

"When brands look for their unique selling proposition, they often don't realize just how much of that resides in their ability to tell a captivating story. If you're not sure where to start (or feel overwhelmed), this book will give you valuable insights into how to think about your brand, and the stories that you tell."

— **MITCH JOEL**, BEST-SELLING AUTHOR
OF *SIX PIXELS OF SEPARATION* AND *CTRL ALT DELETE*

READER REVIEWS

The One-Page Content Marketing Blueprint is direct, straightforward, and simple. It takes all the difficult and challenging aspects of content marketing and simplifies it so anyone can understand.

— CINDY

I would suggest this book to anyone who wants to learn about content marketing from A to Z. Seriously, read this even if you have *zero* clue about content marketing.

— JULIAN

I have read a lot of marketing and business books and this is one of my favourites. I find it practical and realistic. It gives a good introduction to content marketing, prepping you to have the right mindset about it.

— JASMINE

This book does a great job of simplifying the content marketing process and buyer's journey into a step by step guide and map. I've been studying content marketing for a while and this helped me better synthesise and collate what I already know into an action plan while sharing some excellent new tools and strategies.

— TRENT

THE ONE-PAGE CONTENT MARKETING BLUEPRINT

THE ONE-PAGE CONTENT MARKETING BLUEPRINT

Step by step guide to launch a winning content marketing strategy in 90 days or less and double your inbound traffic, leads, and sales.

PRAFULL SHARMA

ISBN-13: 978-93-5406-634-4 (Ebook edition)
ISBN-13: 978-93-5406-923-9 (Paperback edition)
ISBN-13: 978-93-5406-992-5 (Hardcover edition)

DEDICATION

To my father, who inspired me to become an entrepreneur.

To my family, friends, and team -- You helped me gain the skills and confidence necessary to write this book. You also provided constant inspiration and support throughout the entire process. Thanks for your support!

DOWNLOAD THE ONLINE AND PRINTABLE WORKBOOK FREE!

Read This First

I have found that readers have the most success with my book when they use the workbook and templates as they read.

Just to say thank you for buying my book, I would like to give you the online and printable workbook 100% FREE!

Visit leadspanda.com/cmb to download the online workbook and printable PDF.

CONTENTS

ACKNOWLEDGMENTS

There were so many awesome people that inspired me to write this book and helped me continuously improve it.

While it's my name that you see on this book, I cannot by all means take the sole credit for this project.

First, there are a lot of great marketers who inspire me to do what I do. Without the generosity of these legendary marketers to share their knowledge and passion to the community, this book will not be possible.

I want to mention my biggest influences and inspirations in no particular order:

Ryan Deiss, Frank Kern, Dan Kennedy, Gary Vaynerchuk, Russell Brunson, Aaron Fletcher, Brian Clark, Eugene Schwartz, Perry Belcher, Jeff Walker, Brian Halligan, Jay Baer, Neil Patel, and Joe Pulizzi just to name a few.

I also would like to thank our former and current clients at Leads-Panda for giving us the opportunity to do what we love and play an important role in growing their businesses. May we have more successes together in the future.

Last but definitely not the least, my team behind LeadsPanda for sharing your expertise and passion for content marketing every day. I couldn't ask for a better team to work with.

To all of you, my heartfelt gratitude and appreciation.

INTRODUCTION

Before Anything Else...Why This Book?

To say that content marketing is not easy is a big understatement.

It was easier back in the day when content marketing almost solely meant blogging. When there were fewer platforms and distribution channels that you needed to worry about, and fewer businesses who were competing for the attention of your audience.

Proof that content marketing is getting harder is Content Marketing Institute's survey among B2B marketers and how effective they perceive content marketing to be. Only 5% of those who were surveyed agreed that content marketing is "very effective." 45% said it was "somewhat effective."[1]

Yet, content marketing remains one of the required marketing tools that you need to generate traffic, get more leads, and ultimately increase your sales and revenue. This is especially true for small businesses and startups that have very lean marketing budgets.

I feel your pain. I know how frustrating it is to spend hours creating content that doesn't deliver results. I spent years failing and trying again — this is why I started LeadsPanda, a preferred content marketing partner for small businesses, enterprises, and startups.

So, if you've been having a hard time coming up with a content marketing strategy that works, this book could be your first step to reaping the potential benefits content marketing can have for your business.

WHY ONE PAGE?

Surprisingly, this is one of the most common questions that I got when I revealed the idea of this book to my team, friends, and colleagues. I didn't think the length of the blueprint would be something of great interest, but I was clearly mistaken.

Why? I cannot know for sure, but one hypothesis I have is that it's due to the nature of content marketing. Content marketing is not simple -- to say the least. Content marketing has also been around for so long that it has evolved so much. A lot of best practices, tactics, and techniques have come up over the years that it seems impossible to sum up everything in a one-page blueprint or roadmap.

The concept of creating a one-page marketing blueprint stemmed from two primary reasons.

Help Marketers See the Bigger Picture

Here's a disclaimer: Just because the content of this book can be summed up in a one-page blueprint doesn't mean that the information you will find in this book is lacking. As you can see, this book has 19 chapters. So, the knowledge you will gain by the end of this book will certainly be substantial.

However, what I've observed among business owners and marketers is many of them feel intimidated and overwhelmed with the information they find about content marketing. Just do a quick Google search about content marketing and you will see concepts like increasing open rates, generating link juice from high authority sites, increasing click-through rates with attention-grabbing headlines, and so on and so forth. There are hundreds of moving pieces and it's easy to get information overload.

They either get started with content marketing and stop at the early stages once it gets overwhelming or they don't start at all.

Can you relate?

If you answered yes, I created this one-page blueprint with you in mind.

One of the biggest contributors to this feeling of being overwhelmed in content marketing is not being able to see where each piece of the puzzle fits and how the different elements work together. The one-page blueprint shows the interdependencies among these content marketing tactics and how they contribute to achieving content marketing success.

It's a map. If you ever feel lost while going through this book, you can always go back to the one-page blueprint and instantly regain a sense of where you are.

Simplifies Content Marketing into Manageable Pieces

Have you ever heard of the D-Day landings and Operation Overlord that took place at the height of World War II? If not, here's a brief description:

> *"During World War II (1939-1945), the Battle of Normandy, which lasted from June 1944 to August 1944, resulted in the Allied liberation of Western Europe from Nazi Germany's control. Codenamed Operation Overlord, the battle began on June 6, 1944, also known as D-Day, when some 156,000 American, British, and Canadian forces landed on five beaches along a 50-mile stretch of the heavily fortified coast of France's Normandy region. The invasion was one of the largest amphibious military assaults in history and required extensive planning."[2]*

The largest seaborne invasion in history involving 160,000 soldiers crossing the English Channel was led by General Bernard Montgomery. It comes as no surprise that it required extensive planning.

However, here's something interesting. Included in a set of recently released documents from the British Imperial War Museum is a handwritten note by General Montgomery. The *plan* that led to one of the most complex military assaults in history laid out in a single piece of paper:

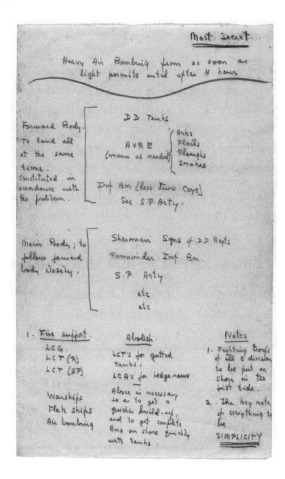

Fig 0.1: General Montgomery's one page D-day plan.

Interestingly, if you look at the lower right-hand corner of the document, it says "The key note of everything to be SIMPLICITY."

The power of a one-pager -- it can launch one of the most brilliant war operations in history or be the backbone of an extremely successful content marketing strategy.

Just like in the military, a one-page roadmap eliminates the confusion out of an otherwise confusing content marketing strategy. It will help guide you and your team to ensure everyone is on the same page in terms of tactics and strategies you need to take to get from Point A to Point B. Imagine if I gave you 5-page, 50-step blueprint. Even the most experienced marketers won't be able to use something so complex.

Just like what General Montgomery said, the key to everything is SIMPLICITY.

So, what's in it for you?

THE FASTEST PATH TO CONTENT MARKETING SUCCESS

When I say this, keep in mind that I am not claiming that you're going to get a tsunami of traffic, leads, and sales overnight. This is not one of those dishonest, overnight success ploys.

Here's the reality: content marketing is a marathon. It takes time and perseverance to get where the successful content marketers are. What this book will do, however, is to show you the fastest way and the shortest route to run this marathon.

It's not a giant read, although it's not a super quick one either. In the next 19 chapters, you will be guided through the different content marketing principles that form the core pillars of every effective content marketing campaign that you see today.

A ROBUST CONTENT MARKETING BLUEPRINT DISCUSSED ONE STEP AT A TIME

Content marketing without a strategy or plan is like gambling. If you're doing this, you're essentially doing content marketing blindfolded or in a very dark cave.

Fig 0.2: Gambling (without content strategy) vs. Targeting (with well thought out content strategy).

With a plan, content marketing becomes scientific; a methodical approach with clear objectives and tactics. Successful content marketers are not gamblers. They are well-trained archers who know what it takes to hit the target, a bullseye.

As robust as this book may be, you will be guided through several step-by-step action plans. You will learn both theories (to give you an appreciation of the overall concepts *and* the bigger picture), as well as specific, concrete, practical, and actionable tactics; all working together to create one big, effective, and efficient content marketing machine.

In each chapter, you will get:

- The 'What' and The 'Why' of a particular content marketing principle
- A recommended strategy and implementable plan
- The immediate next steps that you need to take (scope of work)

- A list of recommended tools to help you implement these content marketing strategies more efficiently
- The metrics and KPIs needed to measure and track your progress and success

I wanted this book to be educational, but also practical. By the time you reach the last page of this book, not only will you have a better appreciation and good understanding of the content marketing success roadmap; but you will also be armed with the knowledge on how to start, and the confidence to actually do it.

STREAMLINED CONTENT MARKETING EFFORTS

One of the reasons that a number of content marketers are not getting the results they want is because they are doing content marketing tactics that are gimmicky. The tactics look good, they sound good, but they do nothing to achieve a set of business objectives.

Have you ever heard of the Pareto Principle? How about the 64/4 rule? Basically, the Pareto Principle states that 20% of your efforts produce 80% of the results you're getting. Drilling down further, 20% of this 20% (4%) are ultra-valuable business efforts, producing 64% of the results.

With this book, you will be able to really zone in on the content marketing strategies that matter in order to work more efficiently and allocate your time and money appropriately.

HOW TO USE THIS BOOK

At the end of the day, I can neither dictate nor impose how you read and use this book. However, based on how I designed the flow and how I structured the information, below is a two-pronged approach to help you get the most out of this book:

1. Master One Chapter at a Time

Read, implement, repeat

This is basically how you want to go through this book, especially if you're a content marketing beginner. When you finish one chapter, make sure that you really understand the concepts that were discussed by implementing them in your content marketing. At the end of each chapter, there's a section called "Scope of Work'" which you can take as the immediate next steps that you need to implement in order to master the tactics and strategies. There are also free/paid tools you can use and metrics that you should include in your marketing dashboard.

Once you feel that you have fully grasped one chapter, go ahead and move to the next.

2. Use It as a Reference Material

If you're currently doing content marketing, you can use some sections of this book as a guide or reference to improve what you're currently doing. For example, if you currently have a blog and you want to focus on that and improve how you write and publish blog posts, you can jump to the blogging section of this book and use the R.E.S.U.L.T.S. Framework in that chapter.

However, I would still recommend that you go through this book chronologically to stay aligned with the structure of the one-page blueprint.

So, why I'm recommending that you go through each chapter, master each section, implement, and take a short break before proceeding?

The 80/20 Principle

Let me tell you a story.

There were two groups of climbers set on reaching the summit of a high-altitude mountain. Both groups started their trek at the same time, but they had different strategies.

Group 1 employed the services of a guide. Since they had an expert on their side, they approached their climb with a clear methodology -- taking things at a slow steady pace, taking strategic breaks in between, and employing other climbing strategies such as breathing techniques to conserve and maximize their energy.

The second group went on a DIY route. They were focused on reaching the mountain's summit as fast as possible. There was no structure to their climb.

At the early stages of the trek, Group 2 was ahead of Group 1 as the latter sustained their slow steady pace and took their schedule breaks along the way. However, as the climb continued, the members of Group 2 became exhausted. At some point, they ran out of energy and resources, forcing them to give up.

Trailing at first, Group 1 eventually closed the gap and caught up with Group 2. More important, they were able to reach the summit, which was the ultimate goal of the climb.

What made the difference?

Group 1 possessed 3 primary things that Group 2 did not: expert guidance, the right strategy, and consistency in execution.

Why did these things matter? These things constitute 20% of the entire climb, but they produced 80% of the results. This is the classic Pareto Principle which states that 20% of the things that you do in life or in business produce 80% of the outcome.

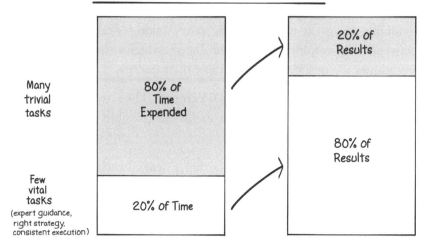

Fig 0.3: 20% of vital content marketing tasks that bring 80% of results.

By mastering each concept in this book, you are also mastering the 20% of the content marketing strategies and tactics that will give you 80% of the marketing and sales results that you're aiming for.

This is the difference between successful and unsuccessful content marketers. Successful content marketers focus their energy and resources on the 20% that matter (which are the principles discussed in this book) but they do it at a healthy pace.

RESULTS IN 90 DAYS

Once again, thank you for purchasing this book and congratulations for taking the first step toward writing your own content marketing success story.

The next 19 chapters will take you through a tried-and-tested playbook for content marketing. You will also get insider info on a unique content marketing framework that has brought my businesses and my clients content marketing success. I guarantee that when you start implementing the strategies and tactics you will learn here, you will have a winning content marketing strategy — that will deliver you results in terms of traffic, leads, and sales — within 90 days.

Read on and enjoy.

CHAPTER 1: CONTENT MARKETING

THE 'WHAT' AND THE 'WHY'

"Content is king."

This phrase has been resonating in the online marketing world for the past few years. Suddenly, what was a "nice to have" became a "need to have." On hindsight, content marketing actually signaled the end of an era: the era of black hat SEO.

Before marketers and business owners focused on high-quality content, it was all about keywords and backlinks. While these are still important, the need for businesses to create useful and relevant content became more necessary as search engines switched their algorithms to deliver a better experience to online consumers.

Online consumers also became more discerning - they like to buy, but they hate being sold to. Traditional, hard-sell marketing lost its charm and businesses needed to find a way to sell without being too "in your face."

Enter content marketing.

DEFINING CONTENT MARKETING

The Content Marketing Institute defines content marketing as "a strategic marketing approach focused on creating and distributing valuable, relevant, and consistent content to attract and retain a clearly defined audience — and, ultimately, to drive profitable customer action."[1]

DigitalMarketer.com defines it as the intersection between advertising and publishing.

Copywriting expert Demian Farnworth offers this definition: "Content marketing means creating and sharing valuable content to attract and convert prospects into customers, and customers into repeat buyers. The type of content you share is closely related to what you sell; in other words, you're educating people so that they know, like, and trust you enough to do business with you."[2]

All of these definitions are on point and have a common denominator - content that delivers results. At LeadsPanda, content marketing revolves around 5 key areas:

1. Content that boosts organic search traffic
2. Content that builds likeability, trust, and rapport
3. Content that attracts qualified, marketable prospects
4. Content that boosts revenue
5. Content that produces measurable results

Content marketing is you speaking in your customers' voice, entering the conversations they are already having in their heads, and providing solutions to their problems and answers to their questions.

THE REWARDS OF CONTENT MARKETING

Business owners always ask: *"Will my business survive without content marketing?"*

The answer is yes.

Content marketing is just one aspect of an overall online marketing strategy and it's not the be-all and end-all of your business.

That said, the more important question to ask is this: *"What are you missing out on if you're not doing content marketing?"*

Here's a short answer: A lot. You're missing out on a lot.

Here are some numbers to back that up.

200 Million Online Consumers Hate Ads

Remember what we said above about how people love to buy but hate to be sold to? There are actually studies to support that claim.

About 200 million internet users around the world use ad blockers.[3] This means that if you're using traditional advertising, you're probably wasting money on something that your prospects won't even see.

Not only that, the number of internet users using ad blockers is expected to increase. Globally, it has increased by 41% year on year, 48% in the US and 82% in the UK respectively.

Enterprise SEO expert Anthony Muller recalls how he started getting annoyed by ads: "If I were writing a confession, I would tell a tale about how I nearly lost my sanity as my mobile phone choked on a 20-slide, "click-bait"-style gallery. It was ever resizing, lagging, and ads kept "enlarging" where the "next" button was located, causing me to click an ad instead of the next button. Yes, this was even on WiFi." He added: "That was when I began using ad blockers on my desktop and phone. Maybe it was one of the first cases of PTAD (Post Traumatic Ad Disorder) ever recorded. I'm getting long in the tooth and don't appreciate having my precious remaining moments sucked up by ads."[4]

With the use of ad blockers on the rise, using content is one of the best ways that businesses and information marketers can monetize their site. In May 2016, Doug Beney wrote an ebook on a niche topic -- how to build a DIY MIDI Controller, a device used to send music notes to a computer to trigger digital musical instruments.[5] Without using any pop-up ads on his site, he was able to earn $3,000 in just two weeks. This underscores that content is a great way to work your way around ad blockers to monetize your site.

Unlike traditional, intrusive advertisements that annoy people, content marketing provides value. Instead of blocking them, online consumers seek them out to get informed, be entertained, or find solutions to their problems.

Sites With Great Content Get 7.8x More Traffic

Businesses that embrace content marketing are able to establish themselves as thought leaders and top-of-mind resources among their prospects. It doesn't come as a surprise that websites with great content get 7.8x more traffic versus their competitors. Businesses that have a solid content marketing strategy experience 19.7% year-on-year traffic growth, compared to the 2.5% traffic growth recorded by businesses with no content marketing strategy.[6]

One good example is Search Engine Journal (SEJ). Over the years, SEJ has established itself as an authority in SEO. They did not do it with paid advertising, but through the creation of high quality, actionable content. As a result, SEJ is now reaping the benefit of having close to 1 million unique visitors per month.[7]

Here's another example. Shane Barker and the team of Gifographics.co were facing a traffic problem with a one-year old website that was only getting about 35 visitors a day. With a 6-pronged marketing strategy, they were able to generate a flood of traffic. According to Shane Barker: "After 6 months of implementing these solutions, I witnessed a dramatic increase in organic traffic to my website. Between June 2017—November 2017 and December 2017—May 2018, the total visitors to my site increased by 80.64%."[8]

Businesses Can Save 62% in Advertising and Generate 3x More Leads

When selling online, the businesses who are willing and able to spend more to acquire a customer win. However, what if you don't have a big bucket of cash to spend on advertising?

Content marketing, once again, saves the day.

According to DemandMetric, content marketing costs 62% less than traditional paid advertising.[9]

Here's more good news.

While saving money on paid advertising, businesses who employ content marketing actually get more leads. Per dollar spent, content marketing generates 300% more leads than traditional marketing.

Great Content Results in A 6-Fold Increase in Conversion Rates

As a business owner, your concern at the end of the day is your bottom line. For many, they don't see how content marketing can contribute to more money in the bank.

Here's the proof that you need.

In a study conducted by Aberdeen, online stores that effectively integrate content marketing into their sales funnels experience 6x higher conversion rates compared to those who don't. [10] That's a 2.9% conversion rate vs. a 0.5% conversion rate. Just to give you an idea, a landing page typically converts at around 1%, so a 2.9% conversion rate is definitely on the higher end of the spectrum.

Here's a comparison to demonstrate this benefit clearer. At 0.5% conversion rate, you need 200 visitors to your landing page to make 1 sale. At 2.9%, you only need about 35 visitors to your landing page to make the same number of sales. This translates to significantly higher revenue for your business.

A great example of how content marketing can help increase conversion rates is what Leadpages was able to achieve back when it was starting. Marketing SaaS company Leadpages is one of the biggest names in its niche, but they didn't start that way.[11] In fact, they started with a very lean marketing team and an even smaller marketing budget. Back then, Leadpages didn't have a huge sales, but CEO Clay Collins put forward a challenge -- "a content team of 4 people can outperform a sales team of 80 people at conventional companies".

So, they did. They rolled up their sleeves and got to work. The Leadpages content team churned out 7 marketing sources, 2 eBooks, 10 case studies, and 8 infographics which they gave out for free. They also created a blog, a podcast, and a weekly webinar covering different topics on digital marketing.

The results were nothing short of spectacular. Their content assets were well-received. In just under 3 years, Leadpages was able to acquire 35,000 customers and was generating more than $16 million in revenue. The following year, it was named the 148th fastest growing company in the United States.

All these content marketing success stories are inspiring to say the least. However, as you probably already know, getting life-changing results from content marketing isn't easy. The road to content marketing success is filled with obstacles and business owners have committed mistakes that jeopardized their content marketing efforts.

THE TOP 10 CONTENT MARKETING MISTAKES AND CHALLENGES

Content marketing — or at least great content marketing — is both an art and a science. It takes creativity and a methodological and strategic approach. Contrary to popular belief, content marketing is more than just writing an article and posting it online. With this misconception, a number of business owners commit fatal content marketing mistakes and encounter many challenges they did not anticipate.

Let's start with the mistakes:

1. Not creating a customer avatar. Oftentimes, content marketers create content for themselves. They create content that they want to read. However, this is not necessarily the content that your audience wants to read. This could easily be avoided by creating a customer avatar which we will discuss in one of the upcoming chapters.

2. Skipping keyword research. A well-written article is useless if your intended audience can't find it. Having a solid keyword strategy is essential to the success of content marketing and business owners oftentimes skip it.

3. Failing to use a content calendar. What to publish, when to publish, where to publish - these are the key questions a content calendar answers. It provides organization and structure to your content marketing. Sadly, many content marketers fail to create a content calendar that fits their needs.

4. Creating content that is not in line with the customer journey. Imagine showing your audience content about your products when they are not ready to buy, or showing them an educational blog post when they are actually ready to purchase. Many marketers fail to realize that the efficacy of their content is heavily dependent on where their audiences are at the buyer's journey.

5. Not producing high-quality content consistently. There are two major shortcomings content marketers commit in this regard. One, those who produce high-quality content but do so sporadically. Second, those who produce content on a regular basis but the quality suffers. Great content marketers produce high-quality content all the time.

Now that we've talked about the mistakes, let's look at some of the biggest challenges content marketers are faced with:

6. Insufficient resources. Business owners who are not familiar with the amount of work content marketing requires find themselves overwhelmed. The next best option is to hire someone to do it. However, hiring capable writers is difficult while many content marketing agencies charge sky high fees.

7. Content burnout. When people order food, it's rare that they're going to buy the same thing over and over again. It's the same with consuming content - people want to see variety. Meeting this need could be challenging for many content marketers.

8. Unrealistic publishing schedule. Many content marketers are burdened by the belief that they should publish fresh content on a daily basis. However, it is better to publish a well-written content piece once a week than publishing poorly written content on a daily basis.

9. Long-term sustainability. This particular hurdle is related to the profitability of content marketing. Essentially, it's about the cost of producing content versus the revenue driven by content marketing. The question of sustainability highly depends on being able to produce content that consistently captures traffic, converts this traffic into leads, and converts leads into buyers.

10. Increasing competition. More businesses are publishing content and it's not going to slow down anytime soon. Marketers are faced with more competition fighting for the attention of their audience. This is closely related to having a solid keyword research strategy to make sure that your content is found by your prospects. It's also important to establish yourself as an authority to become the top-of-mind content resource for your audience.

YOUR NEXT STEP

If you're still not convinced that you need content marketing to elevate your business even after seeing these numbers, then I advise you to stop reading this book right here. Probably, content marketing is not for you; although I will be quite puzzled if that is the case.

However, if the numbers above served as an eye-opener for you, the next step is for you to understand the content roadmap and blueprint, and how content at each stage brings you closer to your marketing goals.

CHAPTER 2: THE CONTENT MARKETING SUCCESS ROADMAP

THE 'WHAT' AND THE 'WHY'

Before jumping into the One-Page Content Marketing Blueprint, let's first look at the Content Marketing Success Roadmap?

What's the difference you might ask.

The One-Page Content Marketing Blueprint contains the different content marketing strategies and tactics and how they build on each other to give you content marketing success.

In this chapter, the Content Marketing Success Roadmap shows you the different stages as you evolve from where you are now to where you want to be. It will help you assess at what stage of content marketing maturity you're currently in based on your current "content marketing health" and the results that you are getting.

Why Do You Need to Recognize that this Roadmap Exists?

There is no such thing as an overnight content marketing success. Anyone who tells you otherwise is either overpromising or a one in a million exception.

Achieving content marketing success is like running a marathon, not a sprint. You need to prepare a long-term strategy that is sustainable, strategic, and results-oriented. According to the Content Marketing Institute, "65% of the most successful content marketers have a documented strategy vs. 14% of the least successful." Content marketing success doesn't happen by chance or magic. It takes a carefully thought out roadmap on how you're planning to go from Point A to Point B.[1]

I always keep this in mind when talking to potential clients. Many still see content marketing as this wonder pill that would magically bring them thousands in new visitors, hundreds in new leads, and dozens of new sales. And I can't blame them, especially startups. Money is tight and sales are sparse. However, content marketing needs time to bake. Take the example of Buffer a popular social media management tool.[2] It took them 9 months of aggressive guest blogging before they had a noticeable lift in their traffic, lead generation, and sales conversion number (more on this later).

So, when a prospect repeatedly says "How soon can we see results?" or "How many more sales do we expect after a month?" or "Is it possible to make the entire process faster?" during our initial call, I usually don't pursue that lead as aggressive as I normally would because I already know that it might not be a good fit. This is because we follow a time-tested success roadmap and most of the time, it doesn't meet the expectations of entrepreneurs who are in such a hurry to see the results they want.

The following roadmap is what we use at LeadsPanda. It provides a clear step-by-step roadmap to content marketing success. It recognizes not only the action steps needed but also the problems and challenges marketers face in each stage.

RECOMMENDED STRATEGY

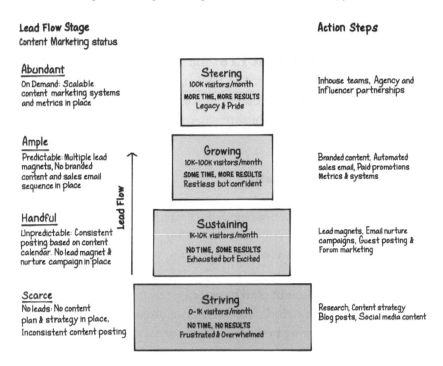

Fig 2.1: Use this roadmap to assess your content marketing status.

This strategy is composed of 4 stages with each stage having different sets of identifiers, content marketing status, and action steps.

I learned this technique from Aaron Fletcher of The Fletcher Method.[3] I tweaked the structure to fit content marketing and to address the needs of small businesses.

PHASE 1: STRIVING

The Scarce Stage

You may or may not be in this stage, but most small business owners and content marketers who are not using any content marketing strategy previously would most likely be in this stage.

Symptoms:

- **NO TIME, NO RESULTS**. You are *frustrated and overwhelmed* at this stage. You know the importance of creating high-quality content in your overall marketing strategy, but you are not sure where to find the time to create content.

Content Marketing Status:

- When you are experiencing Scarce Stage you are getting between 0 - 1,000 visitors to your blog per month.
- You are getting almost zero leads from your content marketing efforts.
- You have no content plan in place.
- Content creation and publishing is inconsistent; you are most likely posting between 1-2 blog posts per month, far below the ideal.

Action Plan:

There is nothing to be ashamed of if you believe you are in the Scarce Stage of content marketing. The important thing is that you recognize that you need to start from scratch and know that you are not stuck in this stage.

Here are the steps that you need to take in order to surpass this stage:

1. **Complete your keyword and competitor research.**
   If you're in the Scarce Stage, there's a good chance that you have not completed the foundational steps necessary to come up with content that delivers positive business results. This includes surveying the landscape and having an SEO strategy in place.

2. **Create a content calendar.** After looking at what your competitors are doing in terms of content marketing and compiling a list of high-volume, and long-tail keywords you need to target, it's time to come up with content ideas and organize them into a content calendar.

3. **Implementation of the content calendar.** Lastly, you need to follow the content calendar you created, posting regularly on your blog and on social media.

In short, your goal at this stage is to come up with a solid content marketing strategy and a content calendar to prompt you to publish content on a regular basis.

PHASE 2: SUSTAINING

The Handful Stage

Having a content marketing strategy and a content calendar are pretty basic elements of content marketing. If you have both but not seeing the results you want, you might be in the Handful Stage of the content marketing success roadmap.

Symptoms:

- **NO TIME, SOME RESULTS**. You are *exhausted but excited* at this stage. You have an SEO strategy and content calendar in place, but you still feel that you don't have enough time to create the content that you need. You're seeing some results, which is enough to get you excited.

Content Marketing Status:

- You're getting some results, but they come in trickles and not consistent.
- The number of average monthly visitors you're getting to your blog or website is between 1,000 to 10,000.

- You're publishing consistently according to your content calendar.
- However, you don't have lead magnets in place and don't have a content nurture sequence for new leads.

Action Plan:

To move past the Handful Stage and move up to the next stage of the content marketing success roadmap, you need to do the following:

1. **Create lead magnets and landing pages.** Offer free content that people can download in exchange for their email addresses. Make sure these offers are on high-converting landing pages.
2. **Create lead nurture autoresponders.** You need to strike while the iron is hot. After subscribing, you need to have an automated email sequence featuring additional content that is sent to your new leads.
3. **Create guest posting and forum marketing program.** You may be getting some traffic at this stage, but you can reach more of your target audience by having a guest posting strategy in place. As for forum marketing, forums are an often overlooked content marketing channel, when in fact, people who participate in forums are some of the most engaged and most active online. You're establishing credibility and gaining their trust if you provide answers to the questions they post on forums.

PHASE 3: GROWING

The Ample Stage

You're seeing more positive results at this stage and regularly getting new leads from your lead magnets. However, you might not be converting these leads into actual paying customers.

Symptoms:

- **SOME TIME, MORE RESULTS**. You are *restless but confident* at this stage. Since you've implemented some automation, you're not as burdened to come up with new content. However, most of your content is educational in nature. You have no branded content and you don't have a sales sequence in place.

Content Marketing Status:

- You're getting significant traffic, anywhere between 10,000 to 100,000 monthly visitors.
- You're getting consistent and predictable results.
- You have multiple lead magnets in place that are constantly generating new email subscribers.
- However, you lack branded content and you have no content-driven sales sequence in place.

Action Plan:

The results you're getting at this stage are already satisfying, but getting leads is not the end goal of content marketing. Below are the steps you need to take to reach the last stage of the content marketing success roadmap:

1. **Create branded content.** This includes whitepapers and case studies that can solidify your authority and credibility in your niche.
2. **Create automated sales sequence.** You need a content-driven sales autoresponder to convert leads into actual paying customers.
3. **Create paid promotions and establish metrics and systems.** How will you know if your content marketing efforts are successful and how do you ensure your content marketing machine is functioning well? This is where you set KPIs and create systems. Likewise, if you want to accelerate your content marketing, you need to invest in cost-effective paid promotions.

PHASE 4: STEERING

The Abundant Stage

The final stage of the content marketing success roadmap and the pinnacle where you want to be.

Symptoms:

- **MORE TIME, MORE RESULTS.** You're producing high-quality content consistently. You are no longer scrambling for time because you have efficient systems in place. You are regarded as an expert in your industry and your content is part of your *pride and legacy*.

Content Marketing Status:

- Your website is getting upwards of 100,000 visitors per month.
- You have scalable systems and can expand your operations anytime because of this.
- You also have scalable metrics that you can use to measure your performance.

Action Plan:

You are already successful as is, but there are a few things that you can do to build on your success:

1. **Build a solid team and agency partnerships.** To keep you at this status, you have to make sure that you have a solid team with you or if you can supplement your content marketing efforts by partnering with a third-party agency.
2. **Partner with industry experts.** If you want to remain the best, you have to partner with the industry influencers and experts.
3. **Regularly contribute to top industry publications.**

Contributing content to leading industry publications regularly will help you strengthen your thought-leadership in your niche.

IT WILL TAKE YOU 12 MONTHS ONWARD TO COMPLETE THE ROADMAP

Looking at the bigger picture, this success marketing roadmap may appear straightforward and short with only 4 stages, but it's not. It can take you anywhere between 12 months and longer, depending on how strategic you will be about it. However, the rewards waiting in the end are going to be worth it.

CHAPTER 3: THE ONE-PAGE CONTENT MARKETING BLUEPRINT

THE 'WHAT' AND THE 'WHY'

J ust to reiterate:

Why one page?

If you skipped reading the introduction, I suggest you go back for a more detailed discussion. However, if you just want to move forward, here's a more condensed version.

Considering all the different elements involved in creating a high-converting content marketing strategy, it's common for business owners and marketers to get overwhelmed and get lost. The result? Marketers start piecemealing different content marketing tactics without even knowing how everything works together.

This one-page blueprint simplifies everything. It gives you a bird's eye view of the entire content marketing process, the different strategies involved, and how each strategy builds on each other. It enables you to see content marketing as a cohesive puzzle composed of several pieces and breaks down the process into small, manageable components.

However, while the one-page content marketing blueprint provides the above-mentioned benefits, it doesn't mean you're going to achieve success overnight.

Following the One-Page Content Marketing Blueprint is a Long-Term Commitment

If you want to be a successful content marketer, you need to be prepared to run a marathon.

Fig 3.1: Content marketing - a long-term marketing strategy (Marathon) vs.
Advertising - a short-term marketing strategy (Sprint).

This is because no one convinces buyers to become customers with a single piece of content (if this is even possible, it's extremely rare). The lack of instant/impulsive purchases is probably one of the main differences between offline and online shopping behaviors.

According to market research expert Daniel Faggella, only 5% of your site visitors are ready to buy.[1] The remaining 95% fall under one of the following categories:

- Approximately 25% are considering your offer
- Around 40% are not yet considering buying
- About 15% are *thinking* about considering your offer
- About 15% believe they're not the market of whatever it is you're selling

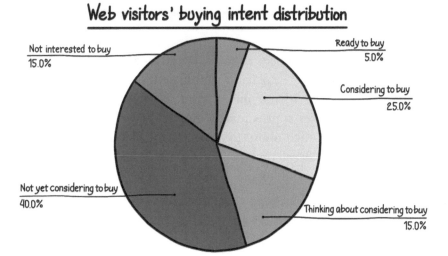

Fig 3.2: Percentage distribution of website visitors based on their willingness to make a purchase.

One of the biggest challenges any business then faces is how to move these 95% of online shoppers from where they currently are to the point where they are ready to make a purchase. This is a process usually called the ***buyer's journey***.

What exactly is the buyer's journey? Hubspot defines it as "the process buyers go through to become aware of, evaluate, and purchase a new product or service."

An effective content marketing strategy should act like a conveyor belt. It needs to move buyers from awareness to consideration to decision. Of course, that decision should be to purchase your products or services. This is called prospect nurturing.

When I launched my first product, I made the mistake of being too aggressive when it came to selling. I didn't understand the buyer's journey, nor did I pay much attention to prospect nurturing. This is the danger new online entrepreneurs and marketers make. I was desperate to make my first sale. At some point, it became frustrating because I felt I had a truly valuable offer and had perfected my sales copy. I didn't see the reality although it was right there in front of me. *It wasn't that my product wasn't good enough. It was just my customers weren't ready to buy.*

In Neil Patel's experience, it takes approximately 6 months for content marketing to "bear fruit."[2] In his estimate he uses a three-pronged approach. Identifying a content strategy and content marketing goals takes approximately one week. Performing an audience research will take about 2 weeks. Lastly, developing an SEO strategy, content development, and content distribution across different platforms and channels takes around 6 months before producing tangible results.

Karl Naim, the CEO of culinary solutions provider ChefXChange shares the same experience. From the beginning he knew that content marketing should be at the core of their customer acquisition strategy. He said: "We have created our blog with the sole purpose of providing free and insightful content to our target audience. You will find recipes, tips on hosting for any type of occasion, birthday and anniversary ideas for your loved ones, and many more. That content is what permits us to be found organically on the internet and building a strong relationship with our target audience."[3] What they found out is that it takes approximately 79 days for online customers to do their research before deciding to buy. Naim adds: "This means that as a business you need to make sure that you appear as often as possible on their radar during that research phase, for any type of keywords they would search for and which are relevant to you."

THE ONE-PAGE CONTENT MARKETING BLUEPRINT

Many experts have defined the buyer's journey as having 4 key stages:

1. Awareness. At this stage, buyers realize they have a problem they need to solve or a desire they want to fulfill. This stage is also called Top of Funnel (TOFU).

2. Consideration. In their own personal context, the buyers define their problems or needs and start researching products or services that can help them achieve their goals. This is the Middle of Funnel (MOFU).

3. Decision. This is the stage where buyers choose a solution - either your offer or your competitor's. This phase is also known as Bottom of Funnel (BOFU).

4. Action. Buyers are finally ready to complete the purchase. For e-commerce businesses, this is when they complete the checkout process. For service providers, this is the part where they sign a contract or agreement. Subsequent actions could include referring additional buyers, creating reviews and testimonials, and repeat purchases.

Content marketer Eduardo Yi realized the importance of aligning content with the buyer's journey after a number of failed sales attempts. "Several years ago, a friend asked me to help him with his new online business—as with most new businesses he needed more sales and customers. I was just starting to learn digital marketing, and I had no idea what I was doing. I read dozens of blog posts and tried every tactic I learned about, but nothing seemed to work and I couldn't figure out why. The product was great, but people just didn't buy. Turns out that I was making the same mistake that everyone makes when they are just getting started. I was trying to sell ALL THE TIME. As soon as someone visited my friend's website, I would try to get those visitors to purchase. I used different styles of copywriting, tried using video, offered coupons...but nothing happened. In retrospect, I can see exactly why that didn't work, but I didn't know any better at the time. What I should have been doing was setting up a marketing funnel."[4]

Based on our interviews and focus group discussions, most of our clients at LeadsPanda start with no knowledge of what they're missing out on without a solid content marketing in place (No Awareness Stage). Then they embark on their own research and are able to read case studies on how content marketing can help them achieve their business goals (Awareness Stage). At the Consideration Stage, the most common solutions that are taken into account include hiring in-house writers, outsourcing to freelancers, and partnering with a content agency. At the Decision Stage, most of our clients realize the cost-saving and other business benefits of hiring a content agency. They come to us, avail of the free consultation and free article, and if everything goes well, sign a contract (Action Stage).

In this book, I will also use the same overarching framework, but offer a more expanded take on the content funnel. I call it the one-page content marketing blueprint.

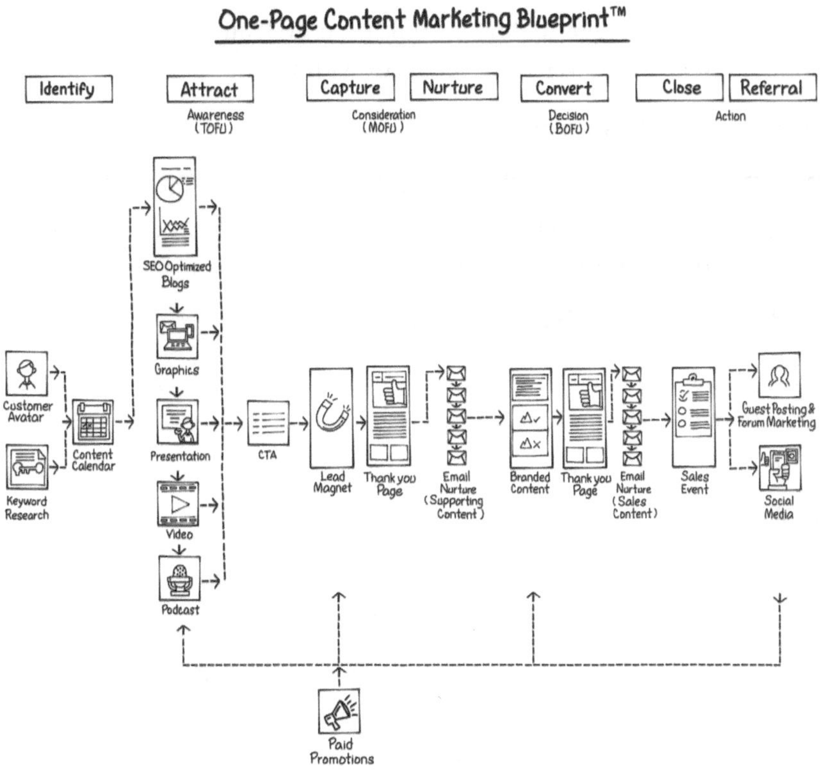

One-Page Content Marketing Blueprint™

Fig 3.3: Use this proven approach to drive prospects through the buyer's journey with velocity and efficiency.

1. Identify

A successful content marketing campaign doesn't just happen. Successful content marketers are great strategists and planners, which underlines the importance of building a strong foundation before any content development begins.

The 'Identify Stage' is the foundation of your content funnel. This is where you identify -- your target audience, what problem they are searching for, and what should you write about. It is subdivided into three tasks :

A. Customer Avatar Development

Consider this as the market research of the process. This is the step when you really get to know your potential buyers to determine what content would resonate the most with them.

B. Keyword Research

A well-written content will be wasted if no one can find it. Keyword research is the process of unearthing what "voice" buyers are using so you can mirror that voice in your content.

C. Content Calendar Creation

This is the process of strategically mapping out your content to maintain a consistent publishing cadence in terms of timing and frequency.

2. Attract

Once you know who your potential buyers are and in what voice they are speaking, it's time to create content.

In the 'Attract Stage,' you're fighting for buyers' attention through your content, convincing them to listen to you. Remember, there are several different brands talking to them at the same time. Therefore, this is a crucial time for you to make an impact, build rapport, establish authority, and gain their trust.

This stage can also be considered as the traffic-generation phase in the content funnel.

Under the Attract Stage, you need search-engine optimized blog posts to ensure maximum reach, while providing value-in-advance (value before they even purchase from you) to your audience.

You will also need to create content in a variety of formats including graphics, presentations, videos, and audio. One great strategy to multiply your content and immensely increase your reach is to repurpose your blog content to other formats. We will discuss this strategy in detail in upcoming chapters.

3. Capture

Once you're generating traffic through content, it's time to convert your website visitors into marketable leads. By getting these potential buyers into your email list, you're giving yourself leverage to send them more content and nurture them from prospects into actual paying customers. Plus, email marketing has shown to convert better at lesser cost compared to other marketing channels.

A. The Lead Magnet

For the 'Capture Stage,' you need lead magnets that give buyers premium content, compelling enough to entrust you with their email address.

Your lead magnet offer should be an irresistible offer, meaning, there should be no reason that your prospects would turn it down, given that it's relevant to them.

B. The Lead Magnet Landing Page

The landing page where people can download your lead magnet is just as important. A conversion-oriented copy is necessary to convince users to give you their email address in exchange for your lead magnet. We will go over this in more detail later, but below is a quick rundown of the elements in a conversion-oriented lead magnet landing page copy:

- Attention-grabbing headline (i.e. benefit driven, curiosity driven, controversial, and has novelty)
- Effective lead (the first paragraph of your copy should convince people to continue reading)
- Bullet points of the main benefits
- Clear call to action

4. Nurture

You also need an email autoresponder nurture sequence to provide supporting content, build trust, and engage your leads while they are still "hot."

This is an important window of opportunity to build rapport and establish trust among your newly acquired leads. Provide additional content to educate leads further about their problem. Make them more aware of the issues they are facing and give them content that provides immediate value a.k.a small wins.

5. Convert

This is the phase in the content funnel where you make your initial move to convert your leads into actual paying customers. In the buyer's journey, this is when buyers have chosen a solution to their problem, and are now looking for a solution provider.

A. Branded Content to Establish Your Authority

At this point, the focus of the content shifts to you, your brand, and your offer. However, while your content needs to be branded, it still needs to be educational and provide value. Perfect examples are branded white papers and case studies.

The goal is to demonstrate how you can solve your prospective buyers' problems without the in-your-face, hard sell tactics. Branded content establishes thought leadership. It also provides content that shows real-life applications for your products and services while building credibility and still providing high-value, high-quality content.

B. Sales Emails to Turn Leads to Sales Opportunities

Similar to the Capture Stage, you also need an autoresponder sequence to further engage buyers and answer any objection they might have.

According to experts, you need at least 6-8 communication touches before you can compel buyers to consider a purchase. Your sales emails provide the required multiple touchpoints and ensure that buyers are aware of your sales messages. As mentioned, it also provides an opportunity for you to address any objection buyers might have that could be preventing them from going through with the purchase.

6. Close

At this point, your leads are ripe to buy your products and services. The content needed at this stage needs to be compelling enough to ultimately make that conversion from opportunity to sales.

There are different ways for you to do this - online webinar, free consultation call, visit to your office or store, online shopping cart, and the list goes on.

7. Referral

In an ideal world, your satisfied customers and people who like your content should be spreading positive word-of-mouth about you. In an ideal world, they should be doing this out of their own volition with very minimal prompting. In an ideal world, you should be getting a substantial amount of traffic from these referrals.

But this isn't an ideal world, is it?

The truth is, while some of your customers and readers will share your content, it's not going to be at the level needed to give you a noticeable traffic boost. Like it or not, but in order to generate a significant amount of referral traffic, your content needs to work harder.

In this one-page marketing blueprint, generating referral traffic is achieved using three main strategies:

A. Guest Posting

Guest blogging or invited content is a time-tested way to acquire referral traffic. By piggybacking on another content provider's authority and network, you are able to tap into a new source of engaged audience.

B. Forum Marketing

Forums and discussion boards have been around forever. Yet, it's only until recently that content marketers have started to maximize its potential. Providing great answers to questions or input to existing threads is an effective way to build rapport with a highly engaged segment of your audience. This type of traffic tends to

convert higher because they are already asking questions or partici-
pating in discussions, which means they are already genuinely interested in a particular topic.

C. Social Media

Arguably the most fertile source of referral traffic, social media
changed how marketing is done online forever. If you're not on
social media, you're practically invisible to thousands of your potential customers.

In the succeeding chapters, you will receive specific tactics and
actionable steps to execute each component of the one-page content
marketing blueprint.

BUILDING YOUR OWN CONTENT FUNNEL

Content marketing success doesn't happen overnight. It reflects how
relationships and communication are carried out in real life - it takes
time to get to know people, gain their trust, pacify their objections,
and finally, build a meaningful connection.

In the next few chapters, I will show you the different nuances,
strategies, and execution plans for each stage of the one-page
content marketing blueprint.

CHAPTER 4: THE CUSTOMER AVATAR

THE 'WHAT' AND THE 'WHY'

I f you asked me back in 2011 who my target customers were, I would have said *"anyone and everyone who needs content marketing."* After all, the wider you cast, the more you catch, right?

I couldn't have been more wrong. It was like throwing empty punches or shooting air balls. In short, maximum effort, minimum results.

When it comes to content marketing, a lot of marketers are too eager to create content (which is not exactly a bad thing) and they make the mistake of jumping the gun, missing out on one important step - creating a customer avatar. Keep in mind that you're creating content for actual *people*. Similar to the real life conversations that you carry out with the people you know, content marketing can only be effective and engaging if you know the audience you're talking to.

So, what is a customer avatar? Expert B2B marketer Ardath Albee offers this definition: "A [content] marketing persona is a composite sketch of a key segment of your audience. For content marketing purposes, you need personas to help you deliver content that will be most relevant and useful to your audience."[1]

Not Just Demographics

One useful thing to note when creating your customer avatars is *they go beyond demographics*. Knowing your ideal audience's age, sex, income, occupation, geographical location, etc. is important. However, customer avatars goes deeper into their psychographics - their likes and dislikes, fears and motivations, wants and needs.

Importance of Customers Avatars for Content Marketers

Why is creating customer avatars for content marketing important? Here are 3 key benefits:

1. Topic Creation. Customer avatars will determine the specific angle that will determine the most effective messages for your content.

2. Get Qualified Leads. Having a clear picture of who your ideal customers are allows you to target the most qualified leads, which makes it easier to convert them later on.

3. Effective Content Distribution Strategy. Knowing who you're "talking" to gives you a clear direction on what form/type of content to create and what channels to use for maximum reach.

FRANK KERN: A PERFECT AND "FREAKY" EXAMPLE OF A PERFECT CUSTOMER AVATAR

According to Jayson DeMers, a prolific columnist for a number of leading marketing and business websites including Forbes and Huffington Post: *"Creating a content strategy without a clear understanding of your audience is a bit like setting a boat adrift without navigational tools. You're out there and you're taking action, but you're not working toward a specific goal. These are the situations that marketers dread: huge amounts of time and money, without a clear potential for good ROI."*[2]

If you've been doing online marketing for a while, you probably know that Frank Kern is one of the most legendary and revered experts in direct response marketing. He also shares one of the best experiences when it comes to proving how having solid customer avatars can work magic for businesses.

For one of his marketing courses called Mass Control (an extensive program about getting highly targeted traffic), he imagined that his ideal customer is Bob, a 45-year old male who earns $48,000 per year selling insurance.[3] Bob's everyday office ensemble is composed of a white button-down shirt, khaki pants, and leather brown shoes plus a pair of glasses. Bob is overweight. He is married and has two kids who drive him nuts. His wife thinks he is crazy to think that he could quit his job and start a living founded on the Internet.

Sounds like your typical audience demographic profile right? Now, here comes the freaky part. When Frank Kern was invited to Orlando to give a talk on internet marketing and list building, he presented how he came up with the character of Bob when he asked the audience to perform their own instant empathy exercise. During the break a man approached him and introduced himself.

His name was Bob. He was overweight and wearing a white button down shirt, khaki pants, and brown leather shoes. He was not wearing glasses. He said he's married and has two kids, although his children didn't drive him mad. He was earning approximately $45,000 per year selling insurance and wanted to quit his job and start his own business online. His wife thinks he is crazy for believing that he could quit his job and generate income from the Internet.

And yes, he bought Frank Kern's Mass Control course a couple of months before the said seminar.

It might be a coincidence that this man's name was Bob, but as for everything else, let's just say it proves how effective knowing who your ideal customers are in marketing.

RECOMMENDED STRATEGY

Later on, I will be providing you with a free source — the content avatar worksheet. The worksheet contains different elements that will make your content avatar a fully realized and fully marketable persona.

Right now, let's talk about broadstroke strategies to help you create the perfect content avatar for your business.

Let's call this the *5 Commandments of Creating a Content Avatar.*

1. Know thyself first. Before being able to know who you're creating content for, you should know who you are as a brand or as a company first. It cannot be vice versa. You should know where your brand fits in your niche or industry and what it is that separates you from the pack. If you know who you are, you would know who to talk to.

2. Thou shall start with one avatar. While one of the main objectives of developing a content avatar is to know *specifically* who you're creating content for, you can actually have multiple content avatars to cater to the different segments of your audience. However, start with one so you can focus on really mastering creating content for your main segment before moving on to other avatars.

3. Thou shall not shy away from research and statistics. In the content avatar worksheet that you will see below, there's no section dedicated to research and statistics. However, this doesn't mean that you cannot use industry benchmarks as inspiration in creating your content avatar. Data such as psychographics, shopping behaviors, media use, etc. are great data that you can take to inspire your content avatar.

4. Validate thy content avatar. While the majority of the processes involved in creating a content avatar consist of ideation and conceptualization, you should validate whether what you created is wrong or not by getting to know your content consumers. Chat with them, hold virtual focus group discussions, task your customer service team to really get to know your customers, etc. A content avatar is just an educated guess until you validate that you're talking to the right people.

5. Thou shall be ready to make adjustments. Your content avatar is not permanent. At some point, your audience will mature, your industry will evolve, and your offerings will change. You should be aware of these changes and make the necessary adjustments to your content avatar.

Now that you know these overarching tips, it's time to get more specific with the content avatar worksheet.

FREE RESOURCE: CONTENT AVATAR WORKSHEET

Nailing your customer avatar is an important element in building a solid content marketing foundation. With so many things to consider, it is easy to get overwhelmed and become unfocused. I am giving you a free content avatar worksheet to help guide you through the process:

CUSTOMER AVATAR WORKSHEET

3. PAINS & FRUSTRATIONS
(What are their biggest problems?)

1. DEMOGRAPHICS
(Who are your ideal customers?)
Avatar Name:
Age:
Gender:
Marital Status:
Location:
Occupation:
Job Title:
Annual Income:
Level of Education:
Others:

5. MAIN PROBLEM STATEMENT

6. GOALS & DESIRES
(What results do they want?)

2. PSYCHOGRAPHICS
(What do your ideal customers do?)
Books & Magazines:
Blog & Publications:
Social Media Groups:
Experts:
Tools (Software):
Brands:
Associations:
Activities:
Opinions, Behaviors, Events:

4. FEARS & IMPLICATIONS
(What happens if the problems are not addressed?)

7. DREAMS & ASPIRATIONS
(What would achieving the goal bring them?)

8. POSSIBLE OBJECTIONS & ROLE IN BUYING DECISION
(What is preventing them from buying? What is their role in buying decision?)

I have also created an online version of the customer avatar worksheet that you can download at leadspanda.com/cmb.

Let's go through the elements of the customer avatar worksheet one by one:

1. Demographics. The first question you need to ask yourself is who are your dream customers? What do they look like? What are their characteristics? Having a clear picture of who your target customer is will help you develop a powerful message and positioning for your content marketing.

Specificity is the key to creating an effective customer avatar. Instead of having a general label, start by giving your avatar a name. This way, you can empathize with your avatar better.

Consider this the bio data sheet for your avatar, listing all the pertinent information about him/her. This includes:

- Age
- Gender
- Marital Status
- Location
- Occupation
- Job Title
- Income
- Other Pertinent Information About Your Avatar

2. Psychographics. The psychographic dimension will enable you to more clearly understand what your dream customers do?

Which media does your audience turn to get the information they need?

Do they watch TV? What shows?

Do they read the paper? Which paper?

Do they listen to podcasts? Which podcasts?

Knowing where your customers get their information will dictate what type of content you're going to produce as you need to tailor fit your content to the media platform.

List out the below information to determine what influences them and where can you consequently go to attract their attention:

- Books & Magazines
- Blog & Publications
- Social Media Groups
- Experts
- Tools (Software)
- Brands
- Associations
- Activities
- Opinions, Behaviors, Events

3. Pains & Frustrations. The question that you need to answer in this section is - what are the biggest problems and challenges your ideal customers are facing that are preventing them from reaching their goals?

This information is critical to connect and engage with your audience, by showing a real empathy for their problems, concerns, and challenges in your content. Producing content that address your customers' problems will compel them to take action to buy your products or services.

4. Fears & Implications. In this section you are going to determine what happens if your ideal customer doesn't address the pain? What does he/she fear?

Understanding the fears and implications will set the stage for developing compelling content that will engage and move your audience.

5. Main Problem Statement. Here you need to determine what is the single most important problem your audience is facing? What is keeping your audience up at night?

6. Goals & Desires. Your clients' decision to (or not to) take action boils down to their level of pain or desire. Under desires, you will need to answer what goals your ideal customer has as they relate to your products and services?

This section will guide you to deliver content which provides the results or outcomes that your ideal customer audience is looking for.

7. Dreams & Aspirations. This section is to discover deep desires of your ideal customers. What is important to them about achieving a goal? What would achieving a goal do for them?

You want to find out why their goals matter to them to find their deepest dreams and aspirations which motivates them to take action.

8. Possible Objections & Role in Decision-Making Process. What would be the possible reasons why your ideal customer won't buy the products and services you are offering? List them here. Also, identify the role your avatar plays in the buying decision (i.e. if you are selling to small businesses, the owner of the business would be primary decision maker).

Now that we've gone through all the elements of the Content Avatar Worksheet, it's time to see it in action.

THE CUSTOMER AVATAR IN ACTION

In order to better understand how the different elements of Customer Avatar Worksheet work, let's take an example of a fictitious Customer Support SaaS company called **Support Hero**. As a brief description, Support Hero provides an all-in-one cloud-based customer support platform/software. The company aims to help small business owners provide a five-star customer support experience to their customers during the entire customer journey.

Below is an example of one of their possible customer avatars. Remember, you can have several customer avatars and you can adjust your content marketing strategy accordingly:

1. Demographics

- **Avatar Name: Ecommerce Eric**
- **Age**: 32
- **Gender**: Male
- **Marital Status**: Married
- **Location**: Texas, but works for a virtual company

- **Industry**: E-Commerce
- **Job Title**: Customer Relations Lead
- **Annual Income**: $88,000
- **Level of Education**: College
- **Others**: Tech Savvy

2. Psychographics

- **Books & Magazines:** The effortless experience
- **Blog & Publications:** eCommerceFuel
- **Social Media Groups:** CX network
- **Experts:** Shep Hyken
- **Tools (Software):** Shopify
- **Brands:** Zappos
- **Activities:** Podcasts, Webinars
- **Events:** The Customer Service Summit

3. Pains & Frustrations.

Eric is challenged with...

- Maintaining a consistent high level of customer support with increasing # of customers
- Streamlining customer service processes

4. Fears & Implications.

Eric's fears are...

- Fear of losing customers because of bad customer support
- Fear of not being in tune with the best customer service practices

5. Main Problem Statement.

Improve customer satisfaction through consistent support

6. Goals & Desires.

Eric wants to...

- Increase repeat purchases
- Decrease product refund and returns
- Improve customer satisfaction scores

7. Dreams & Aspirations.

Eric aspires to...

- Have a feeling of contribution and connection with customers and colleagues
- Be recognized at the workplace and industry

8. Possible Objections & Role In Buying Decision.

Eric's possible objections to the sale are...

- Price point: Can I afford this?
- Learning curve: How long will it take me to master this software?
- Shelf life: How soon until this software becomes outdated?

As customer relations lead, Eric is the key influencer in everything to customer support. The CEO allows him to make decisions for his department autonomously.

You can also download the online version of the Support Hero customer avatar at leadspanda.com/cmb.

RECOMMENDED TOOLS

- LeadsPanda customer avatar worksheet (Download at leadspanda.com/cmb)

- For an area's particular lifestyle and demographics: MyBestSegments[4]
- For polishing your avatar with surveys: Qualaroo[5], SurveyMonkey[6]
- For customer insights: Think with Google[7]

SCOPE OF WORK

- Perform profiling among your existing customers
- Use the customer avatar worksheet to create a buyer persona
- Think of content that would appeal to each avatar

CHAPTER 5: KEYWORD RESEARCH

THE 'WHAT' AND THE 'WHY'

As of recent studies, 92% of all internet users rely on search engines accounting to 1.2 trillion searches done each month around the world.[1]

While SEO is not the be all and end all of content marketing, organic search plays an indispensable, critical role in the success of any content marketing effort. Like it or not, the harsh reality is marketers can easily fall into the trap of *believing that they know* what buyers want instead of *actually finding out* what they want.

You might be assuming that you have a great content idea, but at the end of the day, none of your target customers may want to actually read it. It's like publishing a well-written novel that will eventually collect dust on the store shelves.

Keyword research allows you to base your content marketing on actual search engine data to come up with useful and relevant content ideas, instead of just using your gut to guess what your potential customers want.

Bringing Your Keyword Research to the Now: Understanding Semantic Search

A few years back, SEO went through a dark era of Black Hat SEO. Unscrupulous marketers abused the power of keywords. Internet users relying on search engines were not really getting the information they wanted, due to low quality, spam content.

As a response, Google updated its algorithm to improve search results, ensuring that the content they serve to internet users are those that met expectations. In the past, Google would just string together the keywords used in search queries, hence some of the wonky results that we were getting. But now, Google is able to understand what users are searching for and provide results based on intent rather than just a string of words.

This is called *semantic search.*

Today, semantic search makes more evolved forms of search possible such as more conversational queries and voice searches. This is because semantic search measures meaning and content from the searches, not just look at the search terms. Semantic search is also more fitting today given that more and more searches are done across a variety of devices such as mobile phones and virtual assistants (i.e. Amazon Echo), and the importance of being able to generate search results based on user intent has become more apparent.

Semantic search takes into consideration context to effectively measure meaning and content. Semantic search is also sometimes called intent-based search. Semantic search is also a more fitting algorithm given that search engine queries are now being conducted across different devices in different ways.

So, ten years ago, if someone was looking for a place that sells bagels in San Francisco, that person would probably type a cut and dry search such as "Bagels San Francisco." Today, the same person would probably use Siri or Google Assistant and through a voice activated search say "Find me cheap bagels in San Francisco."

This trend shows in most recent SEO statistics. According to Moz, 70% of all search engine queries are now utilizing long-tail keywords.[2]

RECOMMENDED STRATEGY

Keywords Based on the Buyer's Journey

For content marketing to be effective, it should align with the stage in the buyer's journey where your prospects are in. That said, buyers are using different keywords at each stage and you should be able to target these said keywords with your content.

Marketing Mojo President and CEO Janet Driscoll Miller often teaches search engine optimization to marketers and she underscores the importance of aligning keyword research to the buyer's journey: "I often teach classes on SEO, and I start my presentations off by talking about keywords. When it comes to organic search, keywords form the foundation of all of our SEO efforts. What search queries do we want our websites to show up for in search results? Everything in SEO really ties back to this fundamental pillar. Don't rely on only broad or only very specific keywords and phrases. Instead, consider the buyer's journey when developing keywords. When someone is just starting the journey, searches and questions the person will ask may be broader in nature, but the searches and questions become more specific as the buyer gets closer to purchase."[3]

Many years ago, I wrote a blog post entitled *The Basics of Content Writing:*

The Basics of Content Writing

As more and more website owners and businesses seek out content writers, honing your writing skills becomes even more important. A successful web content writer needs to have certain characteristics and abilities in order to remain in-demand. A web content writer is responsible for providing short and informative pieces on a given subject, usually contracting to write articles for a client.

Fig 5.1: My very first blog posts that did not generate expected results.

It was one of the very first blog posts that I published on our website. Back then, I was doing keyword research like how everyone else was doing it: going for keywords with high search volume. For this post, I was targeting the broad term "content writing."

I had the same mentality that I mentioned when I was creating my very first customer avatar: The wider net you cast, the more customers you catch. As you may have already guessed, this blog didn't get as much engagement nor traffic that I envisioned it would.

Of course, I can just look back at this experience today, laugh about it and charge it to experience. If I'm going to run "content writing" in SEMrush, one of the keyword research tools our team uses, I am going to get the following results:

Keyword ⇕		Volume ⇕	Trend	KD ⇕	CPC ⇕	Com. ⇕	SERP Feat. ▼	Results in SERP ▼
content writing	⇶	4,400		73.72	10.52	0.68	4	2.3B

Fig 5.2: Broad keyword with high keyword difficulty (KD) score.

While it has a decent search volume at 4,400 average monthly searches, just look at the level of difficulty that it would take to rank for this keyword. Also, notice how there are 2.3 billion results that appear for the search engine results pages (SERP) for this broad term.

More importantly, "content writing" isn't cognizant to our company's customer journey. Since it's a broad keyword, it could be something that our potential customers use every step of the way. However, it's not associated with specific customer intent that would serve as a framework for conversion-oriented content development.

I am one of the many content marketers who committed this mistake, but what's alarming is the number of businesses that continue to do keyword research without taking into consideration the buyer's journey.

The following is the customer journey that your keyword research needs to follow:

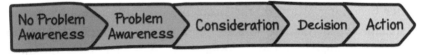

Fig 5.3: Map your keyword research to the buyer's journey stages.

1. No Problem Awareness

This is the stage when your prospects are "inert" or benign -- they are not aware of your brand/company, they don't know about your products and services, and they are not even cognizant that they have a problem.

You might think that you can't do any content marketing at this stage and hence, no keyword research.

Actually, you can. At this stage, the goal of your content marketing is audience development. This means driving the right people to your website who are interested in your topic, and eventually, know, like, and trust you.

At this stage, you are casting a wide net to capture as much traffic as you can. You should focus on keywords that have a high search volume, and low competition.

2. Problem Awareness

In this step, prospects become aware that they have a problem -- but they don't fully understand what it is yet. They also don't know what solutions are available to them. Likewise, they don't know your company and your competitors.

At this stage, your keyword research should focus on the pain points of your customer avatar. They are probably researching more about their problem, creating a perfect opportunity for you to exacerbate their pain. This will eventually push them to look for a solution. This will also allow you to build rapport and trust with them at this stage.

3. Consideration

After becoming aware of the problem, your prospects are now at the stage when they are looking for a solution. The consideration stage, also called solution awareness, is when they are acquainted with possible solution options for their problem. For example, in the case of our fictitious customer support software SaaS company **Support Hero**, prospects could be searching for terms such as "effective customer support software."

Notice the use of the modifier "effective" above. This is important at this phase. People could be using modifiers to find solutions that fit their needs. Other examples are "affordable CSR software" or "customer support software for beginners."

4. Decision

This includes one key element: solution comparison.

If you're in an established market, you will have competition, be it direct or indirect. If you have no competition, that's generally a bad sign, and is generally a segment where SEO is not going to be the best marketing channel. Remember, SEO is a tactic to harvest demand, not to create it from scratch.

This is a part of people's search as well, and you can find these comparison terms and reach those people appropriately. These searches are often (for example) something like "Coke vs. Pepsi".

5. Action

At this stage, people are ready to buy, but they are still figuring out a few things before taking action.

This is a great opportunity to deliver a great, frictionless buying experience. For example, for **Support Hero**, people might want to know about collaboration features and they might be using keywords related to this. Having a page or a blog post that answers questions prospects would naturally ask during the buying process will help a lot.

KEYWORD RESEARCH IN ACTION

Once again, let's take the example of our fictitious customer support SaaS company **Support Hero**. Here's an example of keyword research for this company based on each stage of the customer's journey.

Role of Marketing Triggers in Keyword Research

First, a quick explanation of what marketing triggers are.

Marketing triggers are essentially events or a combination of events that prompt your audience/potential customers to realize a need, want, or aspiration that they need to fulfill, satisfy, or achieve.

In short, these marketing triggers cause your target audience to move to the next stage in the buyer's journey framework.

For example, if you're in the weight loss supplement business, this is that moment when overweight parents realize that being obese could cut their lives short, which jeopardizes the welfare of their children. In this example parents are moving from the "No Awareness" stage to the "Problem Awareness" stage.

Marketing triggers are tied into a goal. In this case, one possible goal could be preparing healthy and delicious meals for the family.

Understanding your content avatar's marketing triggers is important for keyword research. Why? Because the keywords or search terms that they will use to help them achieve their goals depend on which marketing triggers created their awareness.

Now, that we've defined what marketing triggers are, here's an example of how a keyword research would be carried out for our fictitious customer support SaaS company **Support Hero**:

1. No Awareness

What The Prospects Are Searching For (Marketing Triggers):

General topics about customer support that are top of mind for prospects.

Possible Target Keywords:

- "customer support best practices"
- "customer support dos and don'ts"
- "top customer support companies"
- "customer support guide"

2. Problem Awareness (TOFU)

What The Prospects Are Searching For (Marketing Triggers):

Pain points and road blocks:

- Maintaining a consistent, high level of customer support with increasing # of customers
- Streamlining customer service processes
- Fear of losing customers due to bad customer support
- Fear of not being in tune with the best customer service practices

Possible Target Keywords:

- "how to maintain customer service levels"
- "how to streamline customer service"
- "losing customers because of bad customer service"
- "bad customer service"
- "stressful customer service"
- "time consuming customer service"
- "outdated customer service"

3. Consideration (MOFU)

What The Prospects Are Searching For (Marketing Triggers):

Prospects of Support Hero could be searching for and trying to answer the following questions:

- Why should I buy customer support software?
- How much would a customer support software cost me?
- How secure is customer service software?
- How do I integrate customer service software with my current processes?

- How long will it take my team to learn how to use customer support software?
- How will customer support software help my company get more sales?

Possible Target Keywords:

- "business benefits of customer support software"
- "affordable customer support software"
- "customer service software data security"
- "customer support software to improve customer satisfaction"
- "integrating customer service software"
- "easy to learn customer service software"
- "simple customer service software"
- "customer support software to increase revenue"

4. Decision (BOFU)

What The Prospects Are Searching For (Marketing Triggers):

Support Hero prospects could be searching for other customer support software providers such as:

- Zendesk
- Capterra
- HelpScout
- HappyFox
- Freshdesk

There are comparing features of these service providers with the ones of Support Hero. They will also look for customer reviews, testimonials, and how Support Hero has helped businesses similar to theirs.

Possible Target Keywords:

- "support hero case study"
- "support hero success stories"
- "support hero reviews"
- "support hero testimonials"
- "zendesk vs. support hero"
- "capterra vs. support hero"
- "helpscout vs. support hero"
- "happyfox vs. support hero"
- "freshdesk vs. support hero"

5. Action

What The Prospects Are Searching For (Marketing Triggers):

Prospects of Support Hero are looking for information on specific questions (FAQs), features, and topics about the product.

Possible Target Keywords:

- "support hero collaboration features"
- "support hero cpanel login"
- "support hero ticketing system"
- "support hero third party integration"
- "support hero email integration"

OTHER TIPS ON HOW TO PERFORM KEYWORD RESEARCH

There are several ways to do keyword research for content marketing. Here's a strategy that has produced positive results for my business LeadsPanda and its clients.

Tip #1. Create a List of Foundational, Broad Keywords

Coming up with a list of long-tail keywords right off the bat can be overwhelming. The best strategy is to start with broad keyword and topic ideas that you can use later on to develop your long-tail keywords list.

For now, brainstorm all the topic and keyword ideas that relate to your business, brand, or niche. This method is going to give your keyword research more structure and meaning.

For example, at LeadsPanda, we offer content marketing services to marketers and businesses. Our list of foundation keywords could include:

- Content marketing
- Content writing
- Content marketing services
- Blog writing
- Content marketing agency
- Content marketing consultants

And so on and so forth.

Consider these broad topic ideas as your compass that will lead you in the right direction during your keyword research process. Additionally, if you're ever stuck in coming up with this list, ask yourself: "What could be the common phrase that my target audience will use to find me online?"

Tip #2. Use Google's Auto Suggest and Recommendations

It's now time to use your broad topic ideas list to come up with more advanced, long tail keywords. One of the easiest ways to do this is by going to Google and looking at the auto-suggest and related searches.

Auto-suggest is the dropdown list that Google shows when you type a query on its search bar. See example below:

Fig 5.4: Find relevant keywords using google auto suggest.

As you can see, when we type "content marketing" in Google's search bar, it's showing some of the top keywords that other users are typing in.

Another place to look is the related searches that appear at the bottom of a search results page. When we search for "content marketing," Google is showing us the following related searches:

Searches related to content marketing

content marketing **definition**	content marketing **strategy**
content marketing **examples**	content marketing **blog**
content marketing **wiki**	content marketing **pdf**
how to do content marketing	content marketing **agency**

Fig 5.5: Use google related searches to find relevant keywords.

These are some of the best long-tail keywords that you can use in your content marketing.

Tip #3. Spy on Your Competitors

One of the things that you need to keep in mind when doing

content marketing is you don't need to reinvent the wheel every single time. The same concept applies to keyword research.

When The Hairbow Company started putting together their SEO strategy, they knew that keyword research can be overwhelming. To focus their efforts, they honed in on unearthing the keywords that their competitors were outranking them for. They ended up with a lean list of 28 keywords -- a great starting point for a keyword strategy. [4]

If your competitors are doing their own content marketing, there's a good chance that they already conducted their own keyword research. You can leverage this by finding out which keywords they are targeting and how you can use it in your own content.

To do this, you need to use keyword mining and analysis tools such as Moz, Spyfu, and Similar Web. However, keep in mind that most of these tools will give you keywords that your competitors are targeting for their key marketing pages - sales pages, landing pages, and other pages that they might have.

That said, how do you find out which keywords your competitors are targeting for their actual content, say their blog posts?

One thing you can do is monitor their social media pages. You will notice a pattern in how they craft their social media posts as it relates to the content they are publishing and you will get a good idea on what keywords they are targeting.

Another technique that you can use is to look at articles that your competitors have on other websites and determine the keywords or phrases that they are using to link back to their own websites. You can also look at the title of the articles as article titles usually contain the primary keyword that they are targeting. Tools like Moz can make this process faster and easier.

FINALIZING YOUR KEYWORDS LIST: USING THE GOOGLE KEYWORD PLANNER

Now that you have a list of potential keywords that you can use, it's now time to solidify your strategy and finalize which keywords would make the maximum impact on your content marketing.

This means that you need data to back your strategy up.

Enter the Google Keyword Planner. While there are other tools in the market that you can use (most of them are premium services that you need to pay for), they all just really pull their data from Google Keyword Planner. Why not go straight to the primary source of information?

The first thing you need to do is to create a Google Adwords account, which doesn't necessarily mean that you would be spending money on paid ads. You're just creating one to get accurate data that will help you determine the best keywords to use for your content marketing.

When using the Google Keyword Planner, you would want to look out for the following numbers and what they mean to your keyword strategy:

1. Search Volume. This is the number of searches being conducted for that keyword every month. Here's how search volume can impact your keyword strategy:

- While you might want to use keywords that have a high monthly search volume, keep in mind that it's also more difficult to rank for these keywords.
- Take note of negative keywords or keywords that you don't want to rank for in search engines. Not using negative keywords may actually make the search volume higher than the actual number of users that are using them.
- Aside from volume, look at the trend. If the volume is going down for a certain keyword, it may mean that users are losing interest in that particular topic and it may not be a good keyword to target for evergreen content.

2. Competition. As the name suggests, it's an indicator of how difficult it would be to rank for a specific keyword. Should you shy away from keywords with high difficulty? Not necessarily. A higher keyword difficulty also means higher marketing value, so you can still target these keywords. However, just expect to double your efforts in order to rank for them.

At the end of the day, the secret to coming up with a winning keyword strategy is having a strong recognition that you are writing for real, actual people. If you're able to use their voice, you already have a good starting point to come up with relevant keywords.

FREE RESOURCE: KEYWORD RESEARCH CHECKLIST

To help you with this, I have compiled a handy checklist when putting together your keywords list:

Keyword Research Checklist

1. Get all versions of your customer avatar
2. Map out the customer journey for your prospects
3. Identify what the prospects are searching (marketing triggers) for each stage
4. Get a list of your competitors
5. Determine if geo-targeted list of keywords is important
6. Use google keyword planner to get estimated monthly search volumes
7. Set up a spreadsheet to organize your keywords
8. Look for keywords that have high search volumes and low competition
9. Make sure your keywords have at least 1,000 searches per month

You can also download your free keyword research checklist online at leadspanda.com/cmb.

RECOMMENDED TOOLS

- LeadsPanda keyword research checklist (Download at leadspanda.com/cmb)
- Google Keyword Planner[5]
- Ubersuggest[6]
- WordStream[7]

SCOPE OF WORK

- Identify the customer journey of your prospects and identify the marketing triggers for each stage
- List down possible keywords your prospects could be using at each stage
- Use the tools and checklists in this chapter to come up with a list of your initial keywords

CHAPTER 6: THE CONTENT CALENDAR

THE 'WHAT' AND THE 'WHY'

In this day and age, what hasn't been said about the importance of a content calendar, or its close cousin, the editorial calendar? There are now many versions of this essential content marketing tool, from the most basic to the most detailed and sophisticated.

As basic as it is, the majority of marketers who don't use one.

Including my good friend and industry peer Gary.

"You don't use a content calendar?" I asked surprised during a conversation when we were discussing our New Year's content plan.

"No, I don't." He added: "I don't really see the need for it."

"So, how do you organize your content?"

"I just make a depository of several articles and publish what I think is the most relevant to our readers."

"And how about your team? How do they organize content?"

"They just submit what they write to me."

"And if there are duplicates?"

"I just ask one of them to merge the two."

A content calendar or editorial calendar is one of the simplest tools every marketer *must* have. Yet, many companies from small businesses to Fortune 500 do not have one. Not using a content calendar is a skeleton in the closet of even the most seasoned marketers.

The reason that this "epidemic" exists escapes us, but one theory is that many marketers don't really care when and how often they're creating and publishing content as long as they are doing so. It's also possible that a content calendar can be seen as something mundane that doesn't really offer a big impact in terms of marketing results.

While simple in form, a content calendar is actually an important part of any successful content marketing strategy. It bridges two of the most common problems that content marketers face in terms of content marketing planning:

(1) not having enough content to publish and

(2) having too much content and not knowing what to prioritize.

Smart Content Marketers Use Content Calendars

There are far-reaching benefits to using a content calendar. Here are the top ones:

1. It promotes consistency. Like it or not, once you start publishing content and you start gaining a following, you need to be consistent in terms of timing and frequency. So, if you're publishing two blog posts a week on Mondays and Wednesdays, your audience will expect you to maintain this cadence.

2. You can plan for time-sensitive content in advance. There are certain content topics that need to be published at a specific time for them to be effective. For instance, content that leverages holidays is time-sensitive. Using a content calendar allows you to map out time-sensitive content ahead of time.

3. Align with brand/company milestones. Content should amplify important events such as product launches and new promotions.

In the years of advising companies on how to create content, it has become apparent that a lot of companies miss a lot of opportunities when it comes to incorporating company milestones in their content calendar. Important events such as product launches, anniversaries, key acquisitions, high-profile hiring, etc. should be included in content creation. Based on my observations, even though these topics are "less exciting" compared to other types of content, they do a great deal in terms of building a brand's identity and profile. Just look at how the Silicon Valley giants and other big companies such as Apple do it.

4. Easier collaboration among team members. If you have several members in your team creating content, your content calendar can serve as a collaboration tool where people can add their topic ideas.

5. A record of all published content. At some point, you would want to know what content topics you've already published and when. Your content calendar can serve this purpose. Plus, it gives you a directory of existing content assets you have so you can easily access them if you want to repurpose or re-publish them.

RECOMMENDED STRATEGY

Similar to the previous chapter on content calendar and keyword research, I will be giving you a content calendar template that you can use. For now, we will be focusing on broad stroke strategies that you need to keep in mind when developing your content calendar, whether you use my recommended template or not. Of course, the template which will be provided for you is time-tested.

1. Make sure that your topics align with your marketing

triggers and your keyword research. To recap, marketing triggers are events or series of events that prompt your content avatar to realize that they have a need they must satisfy or a problem they need to solve. These marketing triggers influence the search terms or keywords that they will use when searching for information online.

When developing topic ideas, keep in mind these marketing triggers and keywords and ensure that your content topics are aligned. This ensures that your content avatar finds your content when they're searching online.

2. Try to incorporate your published content as best as you can. If you have time to spare or if someone in your team can do it, try to include previously published content in your content calendar. This will allow you to see where you are in terms of your current content assets. Try to fill in as much of the information needed. Organizing past content into a document will provide the big picture of what you've already done and give you ideas on what worked and what didn't.

3. Give your team access to your content calendar while teaching them how to use it. More than a spreadsheet that documents and schedules your different content pieces, a content calendar is also a collaboration tool. Using the content calendar, you and your team can brainstorm topic ideas. Just make sure that everyone is using the calendar the same way so all entries are consistent. It would be beneficial if you can create a manual or a quick walkthrough video that everyone in your team can follow.

4. Include it in your content marketing process/checklist. This is especially important in the early days of your team using the content calendar. What you don't want to happen is for you not to use it or use it inconsistently. Including the content calendar in your content development checklist ensures that you're using it 100% of the time.

5. Evolve your content calendar. While this content calendar is what we use, it doesn't mean that you have to stick with this template forever. You can tailor fit this template depending on your needs and even evolve it as your content marketing matures.

Now comes the exciting part, building your own content calendar using LeadsPanda's Content Calendar Template.

Let's dive right in.

THE CONTENT CALENDAR IN ACTION

Let's take the example of **Support Hero**, our fictitious customer support SaaS company, to demonstrate how the content calendar works. We will build the content calendar based on the keyword research and marketing triggers per stage of the buyer's journey.

1. No Awareness

What The Prospects Are Searching For (Marketing Triggers):

General topics about customer support that are top of mind for prospects.

Possible Target Keywords:

- "customer support best practices"
- "customer support dos and don'ts"
- "top customer support companies"
- "customer support guide"

Topic Ideas:

- Customer Support Best Practices for 20XX
- The Dos and Don'ts of Customer Support
- Companies that Topped Customer Support for 20XX
- A New Entrepreneur's Guide to Customer Support

2. Problem Awareness (TOFU)

What The Prospects Are Searching For (Marketing Triggers):

Pain points and road blocks:

- Maintaining a consistent, high level of customer support with increasing # of customers
- Streamlining customer service processes
- Fear of losing customers due to bad customer support
- Fear of not being in tune with the best customer service practices

Possible Target Keywords:

- "how to maintain customer service levels"
- "how to streamline customer service"
- "losing customers because of bad customer service"
- "bad customer service"
- "stressful customer service"
- "time consuming customer service"
- "outdated customer service"

Topic Ideas:

- X Way to Deliver Top Customer Service Consistently
- X Tips to Streamline Your Customer Support That You Can Implement Today
- How Bad Customer Support is Hurting Your Business
- X Ways to Deliver Top Customer Support Without the Stress
- How Technology Can Help Increase Support Team Productivity

3. Consideration (MOFU)

What The Prospects Are Searching For (Marketing Triggers):

Prospects of Support Hero could be searching for and trying to answer the following questions:

- Why should I buy a customer support software?
- How much would a customer support software cost me?
- How secure is a customer service software?
- How do I integrate a customer service software with my current processes?
- How long will it take my team to learn how to use a customer support software?
- How will a customer support software help my company get more sales?

Possible Target Keywords:

- "business benefits of customer support software"
- "affordable customer support software"
- "customer service software data security"
- "customer support software to improve customer satisfaction"
- "integrating customer service software"
- "easy to learn customer service software"
- "simple customer service software"
- "customer support software to increase revenue"

Topic Ideas:

- Top X Benefits of Using a Customer Support Software
- ROI of a Customer Support Software
- What Level of Data Security Do You Need From a Support Software Provider
- X Ways You Can Improve Customer Satisfaction Using Technology
- X Things to Consider Before Buying a Customer Support Software

4. Decision (BOFU)

What The Prospects Are Searching For (Marketing Triggers):

Support Hero prospects could be searching for other customer support software providers such as:

- Zendesk
- Capterra
- HelpScout
- HappyFox
- Freshdesk

There are comparing features of these service providers with the ones of Support Hero. They will also look for customer reviews, testimonials, and how Support Hero has helped businesses similar to theirs.

Possible Target Keywords:

- "support hero case study"
- "support hero success stories"
- "support hero reviews"
- "support hero testimonials"
- "zendesk vs. support hero"
- "capterra vs. support hero"
- "helpscout vs. support hero"
- "happyfox vs. support hero"
- "freshdesk vs. support hero"

Topic Ideas:

- How Fortune 500 Companies Use Support Hero
- How Smart Customer Support Managers Use Support Hero to Improve Customer Satisfaction
- X Companies Share Why They Chose to Use Support Hero Software

- X Reasons Why Support Hero is the Best Choice for SMBs
- How Support Hero Stacks Up Against Competition

5. Action

What The Prospects Are Searching For (Marketing Triggers):

Prospects of Support Hero are looking for information on specific questions (FAQs), features, and topics about the product.

Possible Target Keywords:

- "support hero collaboration features"
- "support hero cpanel login"
- "support hero ticketing system"
- "support hero third party integration"
- "support hero email integration"

Topic Ideas:

- Q&A: How Technology is Changing the Game for Support Team Productivity
- A X Step Guide to Getting Started with a Support Software
- Top X Questions About Support Hero Integrations
- Top X Support Hero Collaboration Features Explained
- Questions & Answers on How to Choose the Right Support Hero Plan for Your Business

To help you out, me and my team have created a sample content calendar for Support Hero. Visit leadspanda.com/cmb for an example of an accomplished content calendar for Support Hero. You can also use the ideas mentioned in the calendar to model your own calendar.

BONUS TIP: A CONTENT CALENDAR IS NOT JUST FOR BLOG POSTS

While the linked editorial calendar features blog posts, you can also create separate calendars for your other content assets and content development activities. For instance, you can create dedicated content calendars for guest blog posts, social media content, and video content.

At the end of the day, a content calendar is not just about keeping things organized. It can also bring tangible results. For example, by implementing a social media content calendar, AT&T was able to "guide social media outreach led to a 136% increase in Twitter followers, a 113% boost in Facebook fans, and a Klout score that went from 45 to 61." AT&T's Senior Product Marketing Manager who initiated the use of the content calendar explains: "It's important to have a content strategy which is where the calendar comes into play. The calendar allowed the team to maintain a consistent strategy across multiple channels including social media, email and content marketing. We have learned from this process, and we have also learned the importance of analytics, figuring out when we first started, we were pushing out a lot of marketing content and then took some feedback, analyzed what we were sending and figured out this is not what (our audience) wants. We responded to their feedback, responded to what the numbers were saying, and we changed our strategy."[1]

FREE RESOURCE: CONTENT CALENDAR TEMPLATE

In my years of experience running a content marketing agency, I have encountered different content calendars in all forms, shapes, and sizes. From the simplest to the most complex, from those that are kept and managed on a simple document to content calendars using custom-made apps. Some companies even impose the same branding guidelines for their content calendar as if it's an external marketing material.

You can create a content calendar in any shape or form that you want, depending on what's going to work best for your company. However, I do recommend that you use the following content calendar template. By using this template, you'll never forget any of the major elements, and you'll save a ton of time when producing content.

Download your free content calendar template spreadsheet online at leadspanda.com/cmb.

RECOMMENDED TOOLS

- LeadsPanda content calendar template (Download at leadspanda.com/cmb)
- For researching top performing content ideas: Buzzsumo[2]
- Editorial calendar plugin for WordPress users[3]

SCOPE OF WORK

- Use the LeadsPanda Content Calendar Template to create at least 24 topic ideas for your business

CHAPTER 7: BLOGGING

THE 'WHAT' AND THE 'WHY'

To blog or not to blog?

That is _NOT_ the question.

Blogging is arguably the most quintessential form of content marketing and many businesses are still on the fence about whether they really need a blog or not. There are even business owners and marketers who are very quick to dismiss the efficacy of blogging in marketing, prioritizing "fancier" forms of content marketing.

When I was starting out as a consultant, the one purpose I had in mind was to help businesses create blogs. Of course, blogging was the main form of content marketing back then, but I eventually expanded to other facets of content marketing. Yet, blogging still is and will always be one of the pillars of content marketing because of the benefits it provides.

A Blog is One of the Most Important Content Assets You Can Own

A business blog is more than just an accessory on your website.

CEO Mike Kappel likened a business blog to a salt lick found in farms: "A salt lick is exactly what the name implies. It's a salt deposit that animals keep coming back to—and licking—in order to ingest nutrients they need. Now, whether or not you want your readers to lick their computer screens is up to you, but you definitely want them to look at your blog as a source of "nutrients" they need to return to and consume."[1]

Two Main Benefits of Business Blogging

1. It Drives More Traffic to Your Website

A survey conducted among HubSpot customers found out that companies that maintain a blog enjoy the following rewards compared to the companies that don't:[2]

- A boost in monthly website visitors by 55%
- A 434% increase in indexed web pages
- 97% more inbound links

If you don't blog or you're just letting your business blog collect dust, you're missing out on a lot of potential web traffic.

One of our clients provides online software to help marketers build landing pages. Their business was part and parcel of the whole digital marketing process. As such, the company was not a stranger to how content could help drive their objectives and in fact, had an in-house team of marketers. However, they had their eye on scaling their content marketing efforts and use it to fuel their website traffic —something that their internal team needed help with.

Our approach was three-pronged:

- Develop a content strategy anchored on profitability
- Double content posting frequency to ensure consistent visibility
- Ensure regular content development following a proven process for high-quality, engaging content

With this approach, we were able to increase the organic traffic they were getting by more than 80%. So, if you have a traffic problem, before doubling your ad spend or outbound marketing investments, perform an audit of your blog and make sure that you are producing consistently good blog posts that attracts traffic.

2. It Generates More Leads

Now that you're getting more traffic to your website, you also have a bigger pool of people that you can convert into leads. Businesses that have been blogging have reaped great rewards in terms of lead generation:

- B2B brands have reported a 67% increase in their number of leads[3]
- B2C brands on the other hand converted 88% more leads[4]

The inbound marketing agency led by Oren Smith found themselves in an ironic predicament.[5] They were helping their clients get more traffic and leads, yet they were not getting the same results for their own company. Of course, all they needed was a turning point: "Recognizing the opportunity, our inbound marketing agency wanted to capitalize on our expertise. So in April 2015, we increased our blogging efforts and began publishing three posts per week. Full team participation."

This simple modification -- blogging at least 3x a week -- brought through-the-roof lead generation results for Smith's agency: "Since then, we've seen an increase in blog subscribers by 4,300%, monthly blog post views by 163%, organic traffic by 182%, and visit-to-lead conversions via organic search by 259%. And what's key here is that the leads we're generating are much more qualified to buy and in line with our target markets."

RECOMMENDED STRATEGY - THE R.E.S.U.L.T.S. FRAMEWORK

Now that you know (and hopefully convinced) that you need a blog, it's time for you to learn how to write blog posts that bring you closer to your marketing and business goals.

Needless to say, not all blog posts are created equal.

There are blog posts that are like books collecting dust -- no one is reading them, engaging with them, or responding to them.

The following framework allows you to create high-converting blog posts that deliver *results.*

And you need to remember just that -- R.E.S.U.L.T.S.

Here is a summary of what it stands for:

R – iveting Headline

E – xciting Introduction

S – mart SEO Strategy

U – ncomplicated Content

L – everage Graphics

T – actical Summary

S – imple Next Steps

Before I came up with the R.E.S.U.L.T.S. Framework, we were already getting positive results from the blogs that we write for our clients as well as for our own blogs. However, the challenge was making the formula repeatable, improvable, teachable, and standardized across our team. Based on this, the R.E.S.U.L.T.S. Framework accomplished 4 things for us and our clients:

- We get consistent results from our blogging efforts
- We are able to iterate from existing posts and improve on things that are not working
- The framework is teachable to new members of our content team, as well as to clients who want to move

forward with doing content in-house after their
engagement with us

- Blog posts are created, edited, and screened using the same
standards to uphold a consistent high quality across all
output

So, without further ado, here's how the R.E.S.U.L.T.S. Framework
works and how you can apply it to your own business blog:

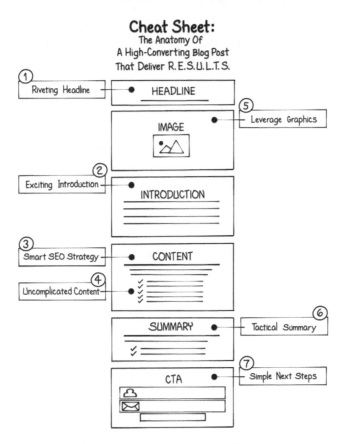

Fig 7.1: Use this framework to double your blog conversions.

R - RIVETING HEADLINE

Eight seconds - that's how much time you have, to capture the attention of your buyers. While the headline forms a small percentage of a blog post in terms of word count, it's arguably the most important.

The headline is the core element in any form of advertising or copy. In fact, I've heard several copywriting experts say they spend a major chunk of their article creation time developing a great headline! This is for good reason: most Web surfers view Web pages and content in "scan mode," glancing over content for anything that stands out.

Your headline should grab your reader's attention and make them feel like skipping your article could be one of the worst decisions they've ever made! Each of the following headline formats is designed to hit certain well-known psychological triggers (such as curiosity, fear of loss, relevancy). These triggers work very well, as humans are often pre-programmed to react to certain stimuli on a subconscious level.

Here are some examples of great blog headline formats that you can follow:

1. Humor or controversy ("10 Things Your Doctor Is Not Telling You"). People will always gravitate to content that makes them smile, even when researching for the most non-comedic topics. On the other hand, controversy will always turn heads, as it connects with sensitive and emotional parts of the brain. Any time you mention an issue in your headline that divides folks, it'll surely get attention. However, be careful what you wish for—to avoid negative feedback, use controversy in a lighthearted manner.

2. Numbered list ("X Ways To…"). Numbered lists are the linchpins of effective headline writing, used often in all formats, both offline and online. Numbered lists work well because they provide the reader with a sense of focus and curiosity.

For example, for an article titled, "5 Simple Ways to Get a Raise at Work," the problems of the reader might include:

1. Not making enough money...
2. Fear of asking for a raise...
3. Fear of asking for a raise and being rejected...

No matter what your article is about, the purpose of its content will be to provide value

or solve a problem for the reader.

2. Point out the risks if they don't read your blog and take action today. The risk is what happens to the reader if they don't read your article and gain the information needed to make a good decision or take the right action.

3. Reveal the promise or the benefits that your readers will get if they read your blog post. The promise is a very short, direct statement that explains what your article will cover. Think of the promise as a succinct description of the benefits your readers will gain from consuming your article.

Let's continue with our "5 Simple Ways to Get a Raise at Work" article topic and create a sample introduction, combining the problem statement, risk, and promise:

{PROBLEM:} "Asking for a raise at work can be a stressful experience. Many employees feel certain it's time for a promotion and/or raise but are unsure how to ask, or perhaps even afraid of being denied their well-deserved increase in compensation.

{RISK:} If you don't approach asking for your promotion the right way, you may end up spending months or longer being paid less than you're worth—or worse!

{PROMISE:} In this article, we're about to reveal three surefire, time-tested methods for asking for a raise, increasing your odds of getting that promotion you deserve, and ensuring that your boss appreciates your value and sees you as an indispensable resource!"

While you're giving out valuable information at the beginning of your blog post, you should also create an open loop. That creates suspense and compels the reader to read more.

S - SMART SEO STRATEGY

We're done with R, we're done with E. The next key element in our R.E.S.U.L.T.S Framework is S, which stands for **Smart SEO Strategy**.

Part of a Smart SEO Strategy when writing blogs is speaking the voice of your readers. This means using tools such as Google Keyword Research to know what terms your intended readers are actually using when they are searching for content online. By doing so, you're not just ensuring that you are getting a significant volume of traffic to your blog, but more importantly, you are also getting the right kind of audience.

For better search engine ranking, always use one of your most searched keywords in your headline. Create a list of the most searched and most relevant keywords and use them alternately when creating your blog headlines.

Lastly, use a combination of short tail and long tail keywords to attract both broad searches for the topics discussed in your blog, as well as those who are looking for specific topics.

We talked about the importance of a strategic keyword research two chapters ago. To recap, a smart SEO strategy for your blog posts would include:

- Using the right keywords/marketing triggers depending on where your target audience is in the buyer's journey
- Using a good mix of broad and long tail keywords

- Using keywords that are getting at least 1,000 searches per month and have low competition
- Using primary target keywords in your headline and introduction
- Using keywords as anchor texts/links to other blog posts in your website

Expert Tool: I highly recommend using the Google Keyword Research Tool when doing your keyword research. It's free. All you need is to create a Google Adwords account and you can start your keyword research right away. I also recommend SEMrush which is a paid tool that we use for our customers.

U - UNCOMPLICATED CONTENT

Now, we've come to the meat of your blog post. In the R.E.S.U.L.T.S. Framework, **U stands for Uncomplicated Content**.

This is the main chunk of your blog post where you can demonstrate your authority and provide useful, relevant information for your readers. Length will depend on the medium you're using, but studies have shown that blog posts that take 7 minutes to read get the most engagement. Also, most of the highest ranked blog posts on Google's search results are between 2,000 and 2,400 words.

Here is how to make the body of your blog post reader-friendly:

1. Make your content highly readable and "scan-friendly". While you want buyers to read your blog post in its entirety, it's no secret that most people are skimmers. They will browse through your post quickly and look for visual cues to check if the content of your post meets their expectations. You want your sub-headers to capture their attention to entice them to read your post's entire content.

Using subheadings also has SEO benefits as it signals Google what your blog posts cover. This helps with semantic search, especially if you use keywords in your subheadings. As a general rule, include your primary target keyword in your first subheading. Also, use H2 tags for easy search engine indexing.

2. Use short sentences and paragraphs. Always avoid huge blocks of text. Use concise sentences and break your ideas into bite-size paragraph pieces.

3. Use bulleted and numbered lists. Bulleted and numbered lists also go a long way in increasing readability and breaking down a complicated idea into easy to consume pieces of information.

4. Use simple words and avoid using jargon as much as possible. If you're writing a highly technical piece and the use of jargon is unavoidable, be sure to use examples so you don't lose your readers.

Expert Tool: I recommend that you use tools such as Readable.io to assess the readability of every blog post you write before publishing and make the necessary changes as needed.

L - LEVERAGE GRAPHICS

All high converting blog posts **Leverage Graphics** and that's letter L in our R.E.S.U.L.T.S. Framework.

Many of the best practices for blog images share the same goal as other forms of content: to grab your reader's attention, add value, and keep them engaged. Here are a few of my top tips to ensure that your blog images stand out:

1. Consistency: Make a decision to either use or not use images in your articles. Your readers will grow to expect constancy in the way your content is presented. I recommend including an image in every article.

2. Charts & Infographics: If you're using a chart, graph, or other data containing graphics, it's important to add value right away. For example, an image labeled "New House Prices in Dallas" showing current median prices for several neighborhoods would stand on its own, providing readers with immediate value.

3. Relevance: One of the cornerstones of all things content-related, relevance plays an important role in the use of graphics in blogs. An article about "3 Delicious Gluten-Free Pizza Recipes" shouldn't have a picture of a gas pump. Don't treat your image as an afterthought, quickly adding whatever image you stumble upon. Be sure your images are relevant to your copy.

4. Images of People and Animals: People and animals sell and grab attention like nobody's business. The younger the better—babies and kittens have been proven to garner more eyeballs than all the market research-driven fancy graphics combined.

Remember, you need to keep your readers engaged as they are reading through your blog posts and there's nothing more boring than a continuous huge block of text. Adding multimedia elements keeps your blog posts interesting and engaging, as well as allowing your readers' eyes to rest by having breaks in your text.

Here are some more multimedia elements that you can include in your posts:

- Videos
- Podcasts
- Audio recordings
- Social media posts
- Testimonials

Expert Tool: A big misconception marketers have when it comes to graphics is they need advanced photo editing skills to produce good looking graphics for their blogs.

Totally untrue.

There are free web-based graphics editing software available like Canva that allow you to design graphics like a pro, without the learning curve of complicated software such as Photoshop. What I also like about Canva is it's pre-loaded with different marketing graphics templates such as social media images already with the correct dimensions and sizes.

T - TACTICAL SUMMARY

T stands for **Tactical Summary.**

A blog post without a conclusion is like a movie without a finale or a novel without a proper ending. The summary section is a short but very important section. This is where you "bring it on home," leaving your reader with a succinct conclusion or take away from your article. This is also where you should use social proof, further establishing yourself as an expert in your niche, and also list additional resources that were not included in the body of your article.

It's important to use all the below elements in your article summary and properly set up the article's call to action.

1. Sum up your content into a concise takeaway. This is a simple one- to three-sentence summary of the article you've written. It should quickly remind the reader of the problem, risks, and solutions.

2. Build social proof and authority. Add one or two quick sentences about your particular expertise on the topic that your article is about. Nothing over the top, just a quick injection of social proof that reminds your readers that you and your business are the best at what you do.

3. List additional resources. In many cases, your short blog article shouldn't be considered the comprehensive resource for the topic being covered. Therefore, the last element of the summary section is a place to list additional resources related to the article's topic. Doing this adds great value to your readers—value that they'll be sure to pick up on and reciprocate in the form of repeat visits, referrals, and patronage.

4. List other posts in your blog. Each blog post you publish is a great opportunity to drive more traffic or rekindle interest in your previously published blog posts, as long as they are relevant and add value to the reading experience.

S - SIMPLE NEXT STEPS

The last element in the R.E.S.U.L.T.S. Framework is **Simple Next Steps**...

Each time you develop a piece of content, it's important to keep the goal in mind. This keeps you focused on the topic and related keywords you should be using, as well as the desired action(s) you'd like your readers to take.

1. Have clear calls to action (CTAs). Many writers make the mistake of leaving a clear call to action out of their content. Even bloggers who do include a call to action at the end of their articles often miss the mark by not being clear or direct enough in communicating the desired action.

Your call to action needs to be clear, direct, and compelling. If you can include a special offer, even better. At first, using a strong call to action might feel uncomfortable, almost like hand holding or overt salesmanship. However, if you believe in the value your business delivers to customers, you should be almost evangelical about ensuring your offers get seen and heard.

2. Primary CTA: Present an opt-in offer to capture leads. For some offers or types of business, phone numbers may not be the preferred contact method. If you're building a subscriber list, the end of a blog post is a great place to position a special offer and opt-in form. The same goes for lead generation forms. Lead conversion is about giving your readers several options for contacting you—options that are placed in prominent positions on your Web pages.

3. Secondary CTA:

A. Ask for feedback and comments. One of the greatest benefits of blogging in a content publishing platform is its emphasis on two-way communication. Your blog allows user comments for every post. While your blog might initially seem like a ghost town, you'll soon start seeing comments, questions, and feedback on your articles. These comments are a great source for leads, information, and additional website traffic (each comment is user-generated content!).

By asking a question at the end of your articles, you'll increase the number of interactive comments. Using our sample article "5 Simple Ways to Get a Raise at Work," the author could include the following call to action: "Have you asked for a raise lately? Please tell us about your experience in the comments section below."

B. Encourage readers to share on social media. Given the amazing power of social media to increase your online visibility, and the increased emphasis Google is placing on "social signals" in their ranking algorithms, options for social shares and likes should not only be visible on all pages of content, but you also shouldn't be shy about directly asking for shares and Likes on your website.

Expert Tool: For CTA, I would suggest you to check out ConversionMonk. Using this tool, you can easily create a variety of high converting CTAs such as popups, sidebar notifications, and web bar. Using this tool, you can boost your conversions anywhere from 2-12%. Highly recommended.

FREE RESOURCE: BLOG CREATION CHECKLIST

To help you out, I have created a checklist below. With this checklist, you'll be sure not to miss any critical components of your blog post.

Blog Creation Checklist

1. I have created a click worthy blog title
2. I have researched reference/sample article to make sure the blog is informative and factually correct
3. I have written the article in conversational tone
4. I have made sure the article delivers on the promise made in headline

5. I have set readers expectations in a brief introduction
6. I have organized article into lots of subheads and sections
7. I have used short readable sentences
8. I have used simple english words
9. I have highlighted key texts
10. I have provided links to 1 credible source for every 500 words written
11. I have linked an existing article from my blog
12. I have provided expert quotes as required
13. I have included 2 relevant CTAs at the end of the blog, Primary CTA and a Secondary CTA
14. I have checked the blog for originality using a plagiarism checking tool
15. I have included 2 data points/statistics from industry surveys and research in my blog post

You can also download an online version of the checklist and keep handy while you are producing content. To download your free blog creation checklist online visit: leadspanda.com/cmb.

RECOMMENDED TOOLS

- LeadsPanda blog creation checklist (Download at leadspanda.com/cmb)
- For headlines: CoSchedule's Headline Analyzer[6]
- For SEO keywords: SEMrush.com[7], Google Keyword Planner [8]
- For assessing readability: Readable.io[9]
- For custom images: Canva.com[10]
- For plagiarism check: Copyscape[11]
- For CTAs: ConversionMonk.com[12]
- For analytics: Google Analytics[13]

SCOPE OF WORK

- Review and master the R.E.S.U.L.T.S. Blogging Framework
- Write two 750-800 word blog posts per week
- Implement the Blog Creation Checklist to optimize your blog posts
- Publish your posts and monitor results

METRICS TO TRACK

- # of visits through organic, referral, and social media channels
- # of clicks on CTAs
- # of shares on social media channels
- # of comments

CHAPTER 8: GRAPHICS, PRESENTATION, VIDEO, AND PODCAST

THE 'WHAT' AND THE 'WHY'

There will be a point when you feel you are running out of original content ideas. Coming up with new topics will take forever and writer's block will hit your team like a truck. I've been there and it *sucks*.

The solution to this is really simple, but it goes against what you assume is the right way to produce content.

In 2015, Buffer ran an experiment to find out what would happen if no new content were created for a month.[1]

The challenge was simple—no "fresh" posts were to be uploaded on their blog. There were no restrictions on the type of content created, but they had to be repurposed from past blog posts and resources.

Bear in mind that Buffer is well-known for heavily using content marketing to grow from nothing to having millions of active users, so a risky experiment like this could be disastrous if things go south.

The team decided to test it anyway.

They repurposed old blog posts into a variety of mediums. Info-graphics, video and audio content, Pinterest images, drip email campaigns—they did everything.

The results?

Buffer saw an increase of 4% in organic search traffic, over 100,000 views on a SlideShare presentation, and 27,597 visits to their landing page from an infographic among a list of key positive outcomes. They gained traffic *and* leads despite not producing any new content.

The takeaway from the experiment is this: **repurpose content to bring in more eyeballs to your website.**

In fact, all the top websites today—your Ahrefs and Mozs—repur-pose everything. Their most read posts are likely to be content that has been the same over the years, only updated to keep up with today's best practices.

What is repurposing, anyway?

Repurposing is the act of turning a piece of content into different formats (e.g. making a video series out of your blog posts). Some argue repurposing is lazy, but that can't be further from the truth.

It works because people take in information differently. I see busi-nesses working *only* on blog posts all the time (which is great), but they are leaving money on the table because there are so many mediums you can use to reach customers.

Case in point: repurposing allows you to reach people like Joe the salesman, who listens to podcasts while driving, or Jane an executive who watches business videos in between meetings.

Do you think Joe and Jane would discover your business if you only wrote blog posts?

Absolutely not!

Just by adding two new ways for people to engage with your

content, you've tripled your potential reach. Repurposing is essential if you want your content marketing strategy to succeed.

RECOMMENDED STRATEGY

Our experiments with dozens of repurposing techniques over the years have resulted in the **ABC (All Bases Covered) Method** to multiply content, a **4-Step** strategy we developed to make repurposing a breeze and extremely effective.

The 4 Step ABC (All Bases Covered) Method

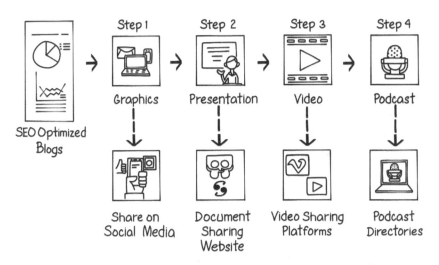

Fig 8.1: The ABC method to multiply your content in 4 simple steps.

This strategy allows you to **4x your reach** and ensures you *never* run out of content to keep up with the myriad of social platforms out there today. The best thing is you don't need to put in 4x the effort to gain its benefits—the formula is designed to be simple so *everyone* can do it.

It involves only 4 factors:

- Graphics

- Presentation
- Video
- Podcasts

GRAPHICS

We discussed the R.E.S.U.L.T.S. Framework earlier and showed how important graphics are in increasing engagement.

Images require another important quality: **they must be shareable on social media**. If you were to take the image out of the article, it must still be meaningful to people who haven't read your post.

Graphics that get shared a lot bring tons of views to the source article. The best case scenario is if an industry influencer retweets your image — your traffic would skyrocket!

This also works wonders in generating backlinks. Not every company has in-house designers for custom graphics. So, the logical thing to do would be to source images from other websites—you want to be that website.

For any graphic you use, there are 2 objectives to fulfill:

a) It must be embedded within your post and

b) It can be shared on its own across social media channels.

Here are 4 simple steps to achieve that:

Step 1: Make sure your information can be visualized

Not all information works visually.

Using graphics to show the percentage of people who prefer sales emails over calls? No problems.

Trying to fit common customer problems in an image? Not ideal.

As a rule of thumb, your readers should understand the information presented just by looking at your graphics. Show, not tell.

If they need to do further research to grasp the situation, your graphic has failed its job.

The best types of info to be visualized include:

- Statistics involving numbers or percentages
- Comparisons between products or services
- Quotes
- Timelines or events

Step 2: Choose an appropriate graphic type

It's easy to clump everything into bar or pie charts. However, you have to consider:

a) Does this graphic type help my readers understand the info easily and

b) Is it easy to create the graphic?

Charts and graphs are best reserved for information involving numbers and comparisons between different timelines, products, or events. If you're selling payroll software for example, you'd use charts to show how much companies in different industries spend on payroll every year.

If you're trying to simplify a concept or tell a story, use infographics. Infographics have the advantage of being long enough for you to put in more content while keeping the graphic to text ratio balanced.

You can use how-tos and instructionals if infographics don't fit your ideas. As their names suggest, use them when you want to educate readers through visual aids.

Step 3: Create the visuals

Don't make the mistake of not having a consistent design for your graphics. Ideally, the colors and style you use should align with your branding. For example, bright infographics would look out of place for a law firm's blog. Yet, blunders like this still happen today.

Do not rely on Google Images to assist your graphics production. Nothing is more embarrassing than seeing pixelated icons and watermarks in marketing assets. Invest in high quality photos and vectors. If you don't have a design team, hire freelancers to do the job for you.

Keep in mind that dimensions for your graphics differ for each social media platform so be sure to resize your images *before* uploading.

Step 4: Share on social media

The final step is to include a social post text to go along with the graphic. It's the same as writing headlines; make it interesting enough so viewers want to read your post after the image captures their attention.

PRESENTATIONS

Some of my clients are surprised when I say SlideShare is one of the top 200 most visited websites globally.[2]

The most viewed presentations on SlideShare easily generate tens of thousands of visits for their respective creators. People use Slide-Share as a resource for articles—especially students—which trans-lates to more backlinks. You could be fortunate enough to land the coveted .edu backlink if a university publishes a study with your presentation used as reference.

Creating effective slides is really simple since you already have blog posts to begin with:

Step 1: Create a presentation template

Like graphics, make sure all your presentations follow a template that matches your company's branding. You can use PowerPoint.

However, Google Docs is the industry standard today thanks to its ease of use and access.

Having a template also avoids repeat work as you can reuse it for future slides. The best templates use easy to read fonts, simple designs, and employ a clear content hierarchy which gives your presentations a smooth transition from the intro to the closing slide.

Step 2: Create and refine your presentation copy

Extract key points from your blog post and summarize them. You don't want your slides to be lengthy, so use bullet points whenever possible. Sentences are fine but keep them short and simple. Avoid filler text and buzzwords since readers are not trying to read an article, they want to comprehend the key takeaways ASAP.

Some suggest the 10/20/30 rule, but I'm not a fan of it. Having more slides is not always a problem; you can present 20 slides in 5 minutes *and* also take 20 minutes to finish 5 slides. My advice is to use as many slides as you need to get your point across effectively.

However, that doesn't mean your slides should be overwhelming. A useful rule of thumb is to **always aim for 3 lines of copy at most with 30pt font sizes.**

Step 3: Use graphics to complement your presentation

Engaging presentations have a great balance of images and copy. You should include an image for every 2-3 slides to create pattern interrupts, causing readers to pay more attention. Images should be used to emphasize key points or explain concepts you can't summarize through bullet points.

Don't worry too much about creating graphics. You already have materials from step 1 of the 4-Step formula. Reuse them.

Images in this case also include inserting your company's logo in each slide. This helps with promoting your brand while discouraging people from plagiarizing your slides.

Important: Remember to include a CTA in the final slide so prospects know what to do next after the presentation.

Step 4: Distribute to document sharing websites

Share your slides on multiple document sharing platforms to maximize exposure. Platforms like Scribd and Issuu are two options alongside SlideShare for you to upload your presentations.

Before uploading the document, make sure the title and filename include keywords you want to target. Many uploaders leave the filename as the title, resulting in gems like *Doc01_final.pdf*—don't do that.

You should also write an interesting description so viewers know what to expect. Too many uploads have blank descriptions which worsens click-through rates. Be sure to leave your company's link in it as well.

VIDEO

You have the blog posts, graphics, and the presentation. Now, we're going to use them as the basis for creating engaging videos.

Why should I make videos? Aren't blog posts enough?

YouTube is the second largest search engine and third most popular website worldwide. It has close to 2 billion active users every month and 68% use YouTube as a way to help them make purchases; that's over 1.3 billion buyers to tap into![3]

Since YouTube is owned by Google, you can rank pages quickly if people like your content and it's relevant to their searches. YouTube excels in promoting top-of-funnel (TOFU) content thanks to its effective video recommendation algorithm and ad platform.

That said, it's equally important to plan videos for other platforms as well, namely the big 3: Facebook, Twitter, and Instagram. The following advice is catered for YouTube, but you can tweak your videos to be used elsewhere.

Step 1: Turn your blog post into a script

Turn your blog post into a script by making it conversational. Reword sentences so they sound like how you'd talk to another person. Here are several ways to make your script more natural:

- Use more *you* and *I's*
- Use informal language. It's fine to include slang depending on your audience.
- Switch things around. The standard blog flow of intro → conclusion is not natural in conversations. Try adding some varieties like mentioning personal stories or advice.
- Cut down on long sentences wherever possible

Step 2: Record your screen and add a voiceover

If you're confident enough to talk to the camera, go for it!

Showing yourself adds a personal touch, especially if the video is helpful and does not feel like it costs a million dollars to produce. Of course, not everyone is comfortable broadcasting themselves to thousands of people, so screen recording is fine as well.

Software like Camtasia and Screenflow allow you to record your screen and audio. This removes the hassle of adding a separate voiceover track. They can also capture specific windows so you can switch to different applications without worrying about recording unwanted information.

Step 3: Record your intro, outro, and CTA along with your topic

Try to keep your videos around 10 minutes. You should have sections for your intro and outro along with short transitions (10 seconds) for both so viewers identify it with your show.

The intro and outro **needs** to be brief. Talk about who you are, what the video is about, what to expect in upcoming videos, and thank the viewers—that's it.

Below is a suggested outline to follow for your videos:

Video Structure

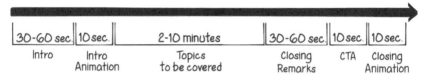

Fig 8.2: Video structure example.

1. **Intro:** Explain who you are and what the video is about (30-60 seconds).
2. **Intro animation:** Have a standard intro animation so viewers can identify with your show and brand (10 seconds).
3. **Topic to be covered:** The main topic and key points according to your script (2-10 minutes).
4. **Closing remarks:** Thank the viewers and talk about the next show (30-60 seconds).
5. **Call to action:** Tell users what to do according to your sales funnel, for e.g. going to your website or watching another video (10 seconds).
6. **Closing animation:** Make sure it is similar to your intro animation (10 seconds).

Step 4: Distribute to video sharing platforms

Your video title and description needs to include your business' targeted keywords since YouTube has its own SEO algorithm. Include links to your website's landing pages and social media profiles in the description box for all uploaded videos.

PODCASTS

Remember when I brought up John the salesman who listens to podcasts while driving?

26% of Americans listen to podcasts, like John, every month. As the average work day gets busier, more and more individuals resort to podcasts as a way to learn new information on the go.[4]

Podcasts are great for promoting content and building relationships with your audience as the personal touch I mentioned about videos also applies. It's refreshing to hear people talk so listeners tend to retain information better from podcasts than blog posts, more so if the guests are excellent speakers.

Fortunately, you don't have to be a Toastmasters champion to create engaging podcasts. In fact, you've already done most of the work if you have several videos under your belt.

Here's how to repurpose videos for your podcast:

Step 1: Extract the audio clip from your videos

Audio tracks of your videos can be repurposed into podcast episodes. By making videos, you're effectively getting two marketing assets for half the effort. This can be done in reverse as well; you can record podcasts and upload them to YouTube or as videos on your website.

Inviting and recording extra episodes are some things you can do to grow your podcasts, but the audio clips alone are good enough to satisfy your audience.

Step 2: Add an intro, outro, and CTA to your main topic

The outline is similar to making videos, but your intro and outro would be a short music track instead. I suggest using something unique so listeners can distinguish and relate it to your brand.

Podcast Structure

30-60 sec.	10 sec.	2-10 minutes	30-60 sec.	10 sec.	10 sec.
Intro	Intro Music	Topics to be covered	Closing Remarks	CTA	Closing Music

Fig 8.3: Podcast structure example.

1. **Intro:** Explain who you are and what the podcast is about (30-60 seconds).
2. **Intro animation:** Have a standard and recognizable intro music so viewers can identify with your show and brand (10 seconds).
3. **Topic to be covered:** The main topic and key points according to your script (2-10 minutes).
4. **Closing remarks:** Thank the listeners or guests and talk about the next show (30-60 seconds).
5. **Call to action:** Tell users what to do according to your sales funnel, for e.g. going to your website or listening to another episode (10 seconds).
6. **Closing animation:** Make sure it is similar to your intro music (10 seconds).

Step 3: Distribute your podcast

Using a podcast distribution service saves a lot of time due to the abundance of podcast platforms out there. Companies like Libsyn and Buzzsprout only require you to upload your episodes on their platform. They'll automatically distribute it to places like Spotify and iTunes along with the episode's metadata.

You can use your website to host episodes, but you lose out on listeners who have their own preferred apps and websites for podcasts.

RECOMMENDED TOOLS

- For creating graphics: Canva[5], Piktochart[6]
- For creating presentations: Google Slides[7]
- For sharing presentations: SlideShare[8], Scribd[9]
- For creating videos: Camtasia[10], ScreenFlow[11]

- For sharing videos: YouTube[12]
- For distributing podcasts: Libsyn[13], Buzzsprout[14]

SCOPE OF WORK

- Come up with at least 3 blog posts you want to repurpose
- Out of the 3, choose the post that is the easiest to repurpose
- Create a few graphics, a presentation, a video, and a podcast episode for your blog post

METRICS TO TRACK

- # of visits/views/downloads to your repurposed content
- # of subscribers, shares, and comments
- # of visits to your website from repurposed content

CHAPTER 9: LEAD MAGNETS

THE 'WHAT' AND THE 'WHY'

Many experts unanimously agree that marketing mimics or mirrors real human interactions and relationships.

Let's take dating as an example.

In order for you to capture the attention of the person you like, you need to put your best foot forward, create the best impression possible. This could include putting on the best clothes, being in the best shape, being funny in conversations, offering helpful advice.

Let's translate that to marketing.

Before buyers form a relationship with you, you need to make an irresistible piece of content in exchange for their contact information so you can nurture them further. This irresistible piece of content is called *lead magnet*.

How Lead Magnets Can Build Your Business

Why is the lead magnet a crucial part of any content funnel?

Remember the old days when everyone was excited to check their email inboxes that they'd be willing to subscribe to just about any newsletter? That time is long gone and buyers are now extremely skeptic before they give out their contact information.

Impact's Tom DiScipio agrees: "You need a Lead Magnet because it makes your job as a marketer easier and more effective. If you were involved in the early days of online marketing, you probably remember when people were excited to sign up for a free newsletter because they were happy to be using email at all. Today, not so much. Although money isn't changing hands, getting the email address of your prospects is a valuable transaction. It converts them to a lead, expresses interest in your offer, and gives you the ability to market your products or services to them."[1]

He adds: "The problem is most people are stingy about sharing their email address, so they have to feel assured that there's something valuable in it for them – which is where your Lead Magnet comes in.

An irresistible Lead Magnet immediately grabs the attention of your buyer persona and delivers real value to them. By winning over your leads with a free offer, you are piquing their interest in your paid offers and starting your relationship on a positive note. On the other hand, an underwhelming Lead Magnet will have the opposite effect. This article will make sure the latter doesn't happen to you."

In short, lead magnets alleviate the skepticism and shows prospects that you are actually someone that they should welcome in their email inboxes. Lead magnets provide results or value in advance. This means that your prospects are already getting something of high value even if they haven't purchased anything from you yet.

The lure of getting something of high perceived value for free is incredibly powerful. Duke University professor and behavioral economist Dan Ariely explained this in his book *Predictably Irrational*. He said: "Most transactions have an upside and a downside, but when something is free we forget the downside. Free gives us such an emotional charge that we perceive what is being offered as immensely more valuable than it really is."[2]

To prove this, Dan conducted an experiment wherein he offered people to receive special deals on Amazon gift cards. The participants had the option to choose from the following:

1. A $10 gift card for free; or
2. A $20 gift card for $7

A simple mathematical calculation will show that the second option offers more value ($13 vs. $10). However, everyone took the free offer. Not a single respondent chose the $20 gift card for $7.

This is why well-executed lead magnets are effective in starting the conversion value optimization funnel for your business. It's a catalyst that converts a visitor to your site into a marketable lead.

Different Types of Lead Magnets

Take a look at the graph below:

Lead Magnets Graph

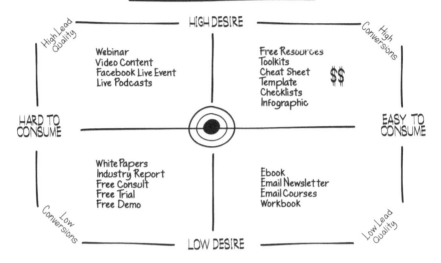

Fig 9.1: Distribution of lead magnets based on desire and ease of consumption.

Essentially, there are four lead magnet categories based on two criteria: (1) the level of desire in your target audience; and (2) how easy or difficult the content of your lead magnet is for consumption.

Let's look at each category:

1. Low Desire, Hard to Consume

Examples of these are white papers and free consultations. These lead magnets would take a lot of time and mental energy for your prospects to consume. At the same time, there's not much desire for these lead magnets due to their complex nature. The result is low conversions.

2. Low Desire, Easy to Consume

Examples of these are eBooks and email courses. These are lead magnets that don't take a lot of time and effort for prospects to use and understand. However, there's not a lot of people who are interested in these lead magnets. Your lead pool becomes smaller so there's a high probability that you will get low lead quality.

3. High Desire, Hard to Consume

People seek after these lead magnets. However, once they find them, there's a friction point as they are not easy to consume. It could take a bit of time investment and some technological requirements on their end. Examples of this type of lead magnet include webinars and video content. The advantage with this kind of lead magnet is being able to get high lead quality, but the number of conversions may not be as high.

4. High Desire, Easy to Consume

I highly recommend that you create lead magnets under this category 80% of the time. There's always a high demand for this type of lead magnet. Further, it requires very little investment in terms of time, effort, and technology for people to take advantage of these lead magnet offers. At the same time, you still get a lot of value. The result: high conversions which mean more leads coming into your marketing funnels.

I would say that if this book was a lead magnet, it would straddle category 3 (High, Desire, Hard to Consume) and category 4 (High Desire, Easy to Consume), depending on who's consuming the information. Since this book is in the long-form content format, it might take a little bit of investment in terms of time. However, it doesn't require resources nor fancy technology to benefit from the information contained in this book. Also, for someone who likes to read and who reads fast, the time element may not even be a friction point. Either way, content marketing is a perennially important pillar of online marketing so the desire for information on this topic has an evergreen demand.

The 7 Key Elements of All Successful Lead Magnets

That said, there are 7 key elements that characterize all high-converting lead magnets.

1. Purpose. Successful lead-magnets should have a single-minded objective. It should provide a clear solution to a specific problem.

2. Focus. Keep your lead magnets focused and specific to a single problem that makes the biggest impact on your target audience, and get more leads among your potential customers.

3. Relevance. Ever heard of the saying "selling ice to an Eskimo?" Even though it's free, no one will take your lead magnet if it's not pertinent to the needs and desires of your prospects.

4. Results. Remember, your lead magnet should be able to deliver results in advance. Your lead magnet should deliver easy and action-able next steps that people can take to reap the benefits.

5. Direction. The lead magnet is only one piece in your content marketing success roadmap. When coming up with lead magnet ideas, you should think about how it will naturally transition into the next step in your content marketing success roadmap.

6. Branding. It's not enough that you're giving out something for free; it has to be of high-perceived value. You can do this by creating lead magnets with compelling design and crisp, well-written, and clear copy.

7. Ease. Your lead magnet should be designed in a way that the content can be skimmed and easily read. People should be able to consume your lead magnet rapidly.

RECOMMENDED STRATEGY

There are different routes you can take to create a great lead magnet, but here's a system that has produced tremendous results for us and our clients. This should give you a seamless and focused journey toward creating your first lead magnet.

1. Identify Your Customer Avatar

Your lead magnet is all about your customers. Sure, you can brand it to show your expertise and establish your authority, but it starts and ends with your customers.

If you don't know how to create your customer avatars, go back to

Chapter 4 of this book where I explain strategies on how to profile your ideal customers.

2. Determine the Main Problem You Want to Solve

After identifying which of your customer avatars you want to capture with your lead magnet, ask yourself this question:

"What is the main problem that I can help my potential customers solve that will make them extremely happy?"

The answers that you will come up with are your lead magnet ideas that you can later on flesh out with more details.

At the early stages of LeadsPanda, back when we were targeting everyone and anyone, we were also trying to solve every known content marketing problem known to man. If we were to cross paths at an industry event a few years back and you ask me what my elevator pitch was, I would have given you muddled statements that could very well be the elevator pitch of every content marketing agency in the world. Today, I can specifically tell you that we mainly specialize in the content marketing requirements of SaaS companies. It's specific, which makes us unique in our niche. However, it doesn't prevent us from getting clients outside of our main target segment.

3. Create Your Lead Magnet's Outline

From your list of lead magnet ideas, pick out what you think would bring in the most number of leads (of course, you can always swap out or split test lead magnet offers) and start creating an outline for each.

When creating the outlines, ask yourself: "How can my potential customers go from Point A to Point B? What are the things that they need to do to solve their problems or achieve their desires, and how can I help them go through these steps?"

The steps you're going to come up with are going to be the backbone of your lead magnet.

4. Create and Design the Lead Magnet

Once you made a decision on what type of lead magnet you're going to create, it's time for actual content development.

If you have the skills to do so, you can write the content of your lead magnets. If not, or if you're too busy to do the actual work yourself, you can delegate to one of your team members or outsource to someone else.

An important note: If you're delegating the actual content development to someone else in your team or if you're outsourcing it, make sure that they understand your voice or your brand's voice. If you're a casual solopreneur, make sure that your content won't sound too formal, as if a CEO of a huge conglomerate wrote it.

Also, make sure that the visual elements of your lead magnets reflect your brand. The color scheme should reflect your brand colors. Graphics should mirror your brand personality. Even your font should be the official font that your company uses.

Apart from being an educational material for your target audience, your lead magnet is also a branding tool.

Your lead magnet should also naturally transition the next step of the content marketing funnel, and that is the bottom of funnel branded content. While the lead magnet provides value-in-advance to customers through practical, useful, and relevant content that helps them achieve small wins, the bottom of funnel branded content demonstrates how your brand can specifically help them achieve their wants or solve their problems.

5. Create Your Lead Magnet Landing Page

Lastly, once you've created your lead magnets, you need a landing page on your website where buyers can enter their email to download your lead magnets.

Here are a few pointers to consider:

1. Use a benefit-driven headline that resonates with your customer avatar.
2. Keep your copy concise. Write 3 bullet points that highlight the key benefits of your lead magnet to your potential leads.
3. Have a clear call-to-action.
4. Don't require fields that are unnecessary. For example, do you really need your buyers' phone number? If not, don't ask for it as it increases friction.
5. Assure users that you're not going to spam them nor give out their email addresses to other parties.

You now have all the puzzle pieces you need to capture leads and increase your email database.

The next step is to drive traffic to your lead magnet landing pages. At LeadsPanda, we recommend a content-driven strategy by creating blogs related to the lead magnet offer and having calls-to-action in these blogs to drive traffic to the landing page.

THE LEAD MAGNET IN ACTION

Using the example of our fictitious customer support SaaS company **Support Hero**, below are 3 lead magnet ideas based on the 3 different marketing triggers that we discussed in the previous chapters.

Take note, all 3 lead magnet ideas fall under the high desire, easy to consume category which will result in high conversions:

Lead Magnet

Fig 9.2: Lead magnet examples for Support Hero.

Lead Magnet Offer 1

- ***What The Prospects Are Searching For (Marketing Triggers):*** Customer Support Best Practice and Technology
- ***Lead Magnet Idea:*** Quiz: How well is your customer service doing?
- ***Lead Magnet Format:*** A quiz/scoresheet where users score their current customer support using a set of questions/criteria

Lead Magnet Offer 2

- ***What The Prospects Are Searching For (Marketing Triggers):*** Reducing Stress in Customer Support
- ***Lead Magnet Idea:*** 5 Emails to Calm Down Irate Customers
- ***Lead Magnet Format:*** 5 email templates that customer

support teams can use to start a productive dialogue with dissatisfied customers

Lead Magnet Offer 3

- ***What The Prospects Are Searching For (Marketing Triggers):*** Using Customer Support to Increase Sales
- ***Lead Magnet Idea:*** 5 Emails You Should Send to Encourage Repeat Purchase
- ***Lead Magnet Format:*** A structure/outline of emails CS teams could send to encourage repeat purchase among existing customers

FREE RESOURCE: LEAD MAGNET WORKSHEET AND CHECKLIST

Use the free worksheet and checklist below to come up with lead magnet ideas for your business.

Lead Magnet Worksheet and Checklist

Lead Magnet Title:

What Value Will Your Lead Magnet Deliver? Describe Briefly Below:

Type of Lead Magnet

High Desire, Easy to Consume	High Desire, Hard to Consume	Low Desire, Easy to Consume	Low Desire, Hard to Consume
❏ Free Resources ❏ Toolkits ❏ Cheat Sheet ❏ Template ❏ Checklists ❏ Infographic	❏ Webinar ❏ Video Content ❏ Facebook Live Event ❏ Live Podcasts	❏ Ebooks ❏ Email Newsletter ❏ Email Courses ❏ Workbook	❏ White Papers ❏ Industry Report ❏ Free Consult ❏ Free Trial ❏ Free Demo

Lead Magnet Checklist

❏ **Purpose.** Provides a clear solution
❏ **Focus.** Tackles a single specific problem
❏ **Relevance.** Addresses a known customer problem
❏ **Results.** Delivers immediate solution
❏ **Direction.** Direct your prospects to become future paying customers
❏ **Branded.** Compelling design and crisp copy that reflects high value
❏ **Ease.** Skimmable, facilitates rapid consumption

You can also download your free lead magnet worksheet and checklist online at leadspanda.com/cmb.

RECOMMENDED TOOLS

- LeadsPanda lead magnet worksheet and checklist (Download at leadspanda.com/cmb)
- For landing page: Hubspot Landing Page Tool,[3] LeadPages,[4] Unbounce[5]

SCOPE OF WORK

- Come up with at least 3 lead magnet ideas
- Out of the 3, create the lead magnet idea that is the easiest to execute
- Create a landing page for your lead magnet

METRICS TO TRACK

- # of visits to your lead magnet landing page
- # of new leads generated
- % leads registered for BOFU content offer

CHAPTER 10: MIDDLE OF FUNNEL EMAIL NURTURE SEQUENCE

THE 'WHAT' AND THE 'WHY'

We've all heard of the middle child syndrome.

I do know a lot of middle children -- colleagues, friends, acquaintances, and the list goes on. Coming in at the "middle of the pack," some of them share the same story of not receiving the same attention compared to their older and younger siblings, while others didn't have the same experience.

Either way, the middle child syndrome is real, well-documented, and is one of the most studied topics in child psychology.

In many instances, the Middle of Funnel in terms of content marketing also suffers from middle child syndrome.

Lead generation is crucial to any business, but it's getting harder to get qualified leads. With people getting a lot of spam in their inboxes, they're no longer as willing to give out their email address or any other contact information to businesses.

So, once you get these hard-earned leads, it is critical that you make sure these leads eventually open their wallets to you and become actual paying customers. However, the statistics paint a gloomy scenario. Business research and advisory company SiriusDecisions conducted a study revealing that 98% of marketing qualified leads don't convert into actual sales.[1]

This is why a lead nurture sequence through strategic content marketing is important. What is lead nurturing? SMB growth expert Doug Davidoff provides this definition: "Lead nurturing is the purposeful process of engaging a defined target group by providing relevant information at each stage of the buyer's journey, positioning your company as the best (and safest) choice to enable them to achieve their objectives."[2]

Here are some numbers to prove why lead nurturing is important:

- Nurtured leads produce 20% more sales opportunities versus neglected leads[3]
- The average order value (AOV) for nurtured leads is 47% higher[4]
- On average, leads need 10 communication touches before converting into actual sales[5]

Business process solutions provider TAB faced a "good problem" -- their sales team was finding it difficult to convert leads to clients because the number of leads they were getting was beyond the capacity of their personnel. According to Ross Nepean, the VP of Global Marketing during that time explains: "The number of leads we generate can be overwhelming for a salesperson. With some campaigns the average salesperson does not have enough time to call or email all the leads they received … That is a wasted opportunity."[6]

To resolve this challenge, TAB's marketing team tested different variations of lead nurture autoresponder sequences. After identifying the best lead nurture email sequence, they were able to increase conversion rates by 32.6%, among other positive business results that they were able to achieve.

Based on TAB's experience, it is apparent that without a content marketing lead nurturing strategy, you're wasting time and money on lead generation. You're also losing a ton of opportunity since email traffic (aka "warm traffic") converts better than other traffic sources.

Here are a few tips to keep in mind when developing an effective lead nurturing campaign using content marketing for your business.

Empower Your Leads to Achieve Small Victories

When your leads gave you their email address, it implies they saw something in your business that could help them solve a problem, satisfy a need, or fulfill a desire. They expect you to continue doing this, even if they haven't purchased your products or services yet.

One of the best ways to do this is for you to create an email sequence that sends them useful, bite-sized content that allows them to achieve small victories. For example, if you're in the weight loss business, you can create a 5-part email series that gives your leads simple, straightforward tips that brings them closer to their bigger goal of losing weight.

What you're doing is showing results in advance. This means that you are already showing them the benefits of your products or services even if they haven't bought anything yet.

This is how Crazy Egg explains small victories: "At its most basic, lead nurturing is about the long con (sans the negative aspect, of course). That is, it's about trying to get little nods of approval that build up into one big thumbs up: your product offer. These little nods of approval are all about building rapport and trust, which is where the mere-exposure effect comes in. The more frequently you expose leads to your product/service, the more likely they'll turn into customers.

Take note, there's a clear line between repeated exposure and annoying users. You want to build trust, not turn your leads off, so don't be spammy. For example, you can link to helpful articles or other content assets related to your offer before bringing them in for your sales pitch. Inform them about your product/service, show them its value, and finally, when you've led them through the rabbit hole, make your big offer."[7]

RECOMMENDED STRATEGY

When it comes to any email nurture sequence, every content marketer needs to remember that in order to drive your message across and move your leads into the next stage of the funnel, you need several email touchpoints. That's why it's called a nurture sequence.

The order in which the emails will be sent out should follow solid marketing logic, meaning, each email naturally leads to and builds on the other emails in the sequence.

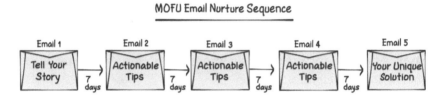

Fig 10.1: 5-part email sequence for middle of funnel traffic.

Email 1: Tell Your Story

After opting in for your lead magnet, the first role of your MOFU email nurture sequence is to indoctrinate your leads as to who you are as a brand, company, or business. Your first email should be able to narrate very concisely your "genesis story" and why you're doing what you're doing.

You would be surprised how many of your email subscribers would appreciate knowing your story, getting a better understanding of who you are as a business, and just building a more personal relationship with your business and your brand.

MeasurementMarketing.io is a good example of a company that does this well. The first email that new email subscribers receive includes a photo of the company's founder Chris Mercer and his wife enjoying a meal at one of the most famous barbecue joints in Austin, Texas where they reside. Right off the bat, they are able to build rapport with their leads by telling the story of their company as well as their personal story.

Emails 2, 3, and 4: Supporting Content Featuring Actionable Tips

For the next 3 emails, identify 3 sub-problems of your customers that you can immediately address and help them with. You can either create premium downloadable content and provide the links in these 3 emails. If the solution is simple enough that a quick step-by-step can be provided in the emails themselves, that is also an option.

Email 5: Expound on Your Unique Solution/ Transition to BOFU Branded Content

For the last email, you need to provide a smooth transition into the next stage of the content marketing funnel, which is the BOFU (Bottom of Funnel) Branded Content. This is where the messaging shifts from educational to transactional. By expounding on your unique solution, you can still provide valuable information, but at the same time, start the transition into a more sales-oriented content.

THE MOFU EMAIL NURTURE SEQUENCE IN ACTION

To give you a better idea on how this email structure and logic works, we're going to apply it to our fictitious customer support SaaS company, **Support Hero**. Below are the 3 questions that potential customers might be asking, which we will, later on, address in emails 2, 3 and 4 in the sequence:

1. How do I know the quality of my customer support?
2. How do I know if I need customer support software?

3. What are the things I should look for in customer support software?

Email 1

- **Sent on:** Day 1 (Immediately after the user downloads the lead magnet)
- **Email Idea:** Welcome to Support Hero: Let's Get to Know Each Other

Email 2

- **Sent on:** Day 4
- **Email Idea:** FREE TOOL: How to Diagnose Your "Customer Support Health"

Email 3

- **Sent on:** Day 7
- **Email Idea:** How Do You Know if It's Time to Get a Customer Support Software

Email 4

- **Sent on:** Day 10
- **Email Idea:** FREE CHECKLIST: How to Choose a Customer Support Software

Email 5

- **Sent on:** Day 13
- **Email Idea:** Be the Hero for Your Customers: The Support Hero Promise

This is how the MOFU Email Nurture Sequence will look like:

MOFU Email Nurture Execution

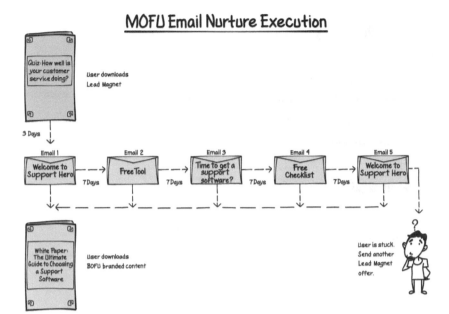

Fig 10.2: Middle of funnel email nurture sequence example for Support Hero.

To make it easy for you, I have created a sample email calendar for Support Hero. Go to leadspanda.com/cmb for an example of an accomplished email nurture planning calendar for Support Hero.

Test and Evolve Your Lead Nurture Strategy

While there are a ton of best practices out there, not all lead nurture content marketing techniques will bring you positive results. As you understand your leads better and as you change your sales funnels, you also need to adjust your lead nurture content marketing strategies.

FREE RESOURCE: MOFU EMAIL NURTURE SEQUENCE PLANNING TEMPLATE

To plan out the content of your MOFU Email Nurture Sequence, download your free online template at leadspanda.com/cmb.

RECOMMENDED TOOLS

- LeadsPanda MOFU email nurture planning template (Download at leadspanda.com/cmb)
- Email Marketing Tool: MailChimp,[8] Aweber,[9] Infusionsoft[10]

SCOPE OF WORK

- Identify 3 questions or pain points your leads have
- Plan out an email nurture sequence with 5 emails
- Write and execute the 5 emails

METRICS TO TRACK

- Email Open Rate
- Click Through Rate
- Opt-out Rate
- Conversion rate from MOFU to BOFU

CHAPTER 11: BOTTOM OF FUNNEL BRANDED CONTENT

THE 'WHAT' AND THE 'WHY'

"**W**hen are we going to start seeing a spike in our sales?,"
one prospective client asked during our free consultation call.

"Well, it really depends on your sales lifecycle because every business
is unique. But, we typically see results between 6 to 12 months," I
replied.

"That long?," he asked, a little bit surprised.

"Well, content marketing is not a sprint, it's more of a marathon.
You need to be prepared to be in it for the long haul," I explained.

"Yeah, but what if we just want to increase our sales? Can we just
expedite the process?"

Silence on my end.

"What if we skip everything else and just go right into the sales
process?"

"I see where you're coming from, but even at that stage, you still need a series of content to convert leads into actual paying customers."

"Really? What if we just create several sales pages?"

This is one of the most challenging conversations I had with a prospect. At the 10th minute mark of that call, I already knew that it's going to be difficult to close this client and on hindsight, I believe it would have been a rocky relationship.

At the end of the day, the ultimate goal of content marketing is to help move sales, especially because money in the bank remains the truest measure of ROI. However, even the process of closing the deal still involves a series of content pieces built on each other and working together to get the sale.

The Bottom of the Funnel is Still Content-Driven

After sending your leads a series of emails, at this point, you need to filter those who just opted into your email list to get the "free stuff" and those who are genuinely considering buying your products or services.

The Bottom of Funnel (BOFU) branded content plays a crucial role in this segmentation. At this point, the focus shifts from just providing buyers with educational content to establishing yourself as their first option when they are ready to buy. When your leads consume content that is "all about you," you're stepping up your relationship with them from being a content provider to a solutions provider.

Branded, But Still Relevant and Useful

A quick caveat.

Your BOFU branded content is not a brochure about your products and services. It's neither a company profile nor a list of your credentials. As its name implies, branded content is still content — relevant, useful and educational – but written from your company's point of view and using your previous work as examples and proof to strengthen your claim.

RECOMMENDED STRATEGY

A BOFU Branded Content can take many forms which will be discussed later. There are, however, a few crucial elements that form the core or outline of an effective BOFU Branded Content offer.

Below are those elements:

1. Build trust by demonstrating that you understand your customers' problems and that you have the capacity to help them solve these problems.

In this section, your BOFU branded content should be able to answer 3 main points:

- What industries or business categories has your brand been involved in? If your customers are individuals, what common characteristics do they share with your other customers?
- What are their challenges and how can you solve them?
- What is your track record in solving these types of problems? How long have you been doing it? What evidence can you present to prove your success?

2. Introduce the specific approach or plan that you recommend to solve their problems.

One book that I read recently that made a significant impact on my digital marketing perspective is *Building Your StoryBrand: Clarify Your Message So Customers Will Listen* by Donald Miller.

He wrote: "The customer is the hero of the story, not your brand. When we position our customers as the hero and ourselves as a guide, we will be recognized as a trusted resource to help them overcome their challenges. Positioning the customer as the hero in the story is more than just good manners; it's also good business. Communication expert Nancy Duarte has done extensive research on how to create powerful presentations. The strategy she recommends to her clients is simple: when giving a speech, position yourself as Yoda and your audience as Luke Skywalker. It's a small but powerful shift that honors the journey of the audience and positions us as a leader providing wisdom products, and services our audience needs in order to thrive."[1]

When I started out, one of the goals was to become one of the most respected content marketing consultants in the world. This dictated how I presented myself and the agency during industry events and even during client interactions. It wasn't really ego. I just felt that if I am going to help these businesses transform their content marketing into real profit centers for their companies, I deserve the credit and recognition.

Obviously, I was wrong.

As a guide to the heroes (aka your customers), you need to offer them a plan or a framework on how you would solve their problems; a unique solution that you're proposing. This solution needs to have a name or a label for you to be able to claim ownership.

The following are the most important questions that you need to answer in this section:

- How would you summarize this unique solution? What is your elevator pitch?
- Why is your unique solution better than a DIY approach or the other alternatives available?
- What are the possible objections that customers might have against the solution you're proposing? How would you address these objections?

3. List your services/products/solutions

More specifically, this segment should answer the following questions:

- What benefits does your product provide for your customers? Describe how each fits in the overall roadmap for your customers' success.
- How is your brand unique compared to your competitors? Why should they choose you?

4. Provide a clear call to action

One of the most fatal mistakes brands make is they assume customers know how to engage in business with them. If you want them to buy, tell them to "Buy Now." If you want them to schedule a free consultation, tell them to "Call Now." If you want them to avail of your free trial, tell them to "Start Your Free Trial."

Customers need to be compelled and told exactly what to do next in order for them to action.

The Different Types of BOFU Branded Content

As mentioned, the BOFU Branded Content can take many forms. For starters, here are a few expert-tested executions that you can implement:

1. Whitepapers. A whitepaper is an authoritative and in-depth report on a specific topic or issue. A whitepaper defines a problem and provides a proposed solution. A whitepaper is an effective BOFU branded content as it demonstrates your authority and expertise. At the same time, it allows you to position your products/services as the best solution to a problem your customers might be facing.

2. Case Studies. Telling the story of how your products/services have helped other people is a great way to demonstrate your credibility as a company and establishing the efficacy of your offerings. What makes case studies powerful is they combine quantitative and qualitative proof from customers you've helped.

3. Buyer's Guides and Product Comparison Guides. An educated customer is a better customer. They know what they're looking for and they make better decisions. You can empower your prospective customers to be smarter consumers by creating buyer's guides and product comparisons. They are more likely to purchase from you because you were the one who guided them through their journey.

4. FAQs. Similarly, a customer who is ready to buy would have several questions that need to be addressed before purchasing. Creating content around FAQs will help your leads overcome any questions or objections they might have and persuade them to finally make the purchase.

5. Product Tours. Think of it as selling a house. Before closing a sale, real estate agents need to do open houses and tours to help buyers envision themselves living in that home. With product tours, you're helping your leads what they could achieve if they buy your products/services.

THE BOFU BRANDED CONTENT IN ACTION

To help you visualize how BOFU Branded Content could be executed for your own content marketing funnel, here are 3 BOFU Branded Content ideas/concepts for our fictitious customer support SaaS company, Support Hero:

BOFU Branded Content

Fig 11.1: Branded content example for Support Hero.

BOFU Branded Offer 1

- ***What The Prospects Are Searching For (Marketing Triggers):*** How Support Hero software is different from other solutions?
- ***Idea:*** The Ultimate Guide To Choosing a Support Software
- ***Format:*** An exclusive whitepaper to position Support Hero's unique solution as the preferred solution of brands who love their customers

BOFU Branded Offer 2

- ***What The Prospects Are Searching For (Marketing Triggers):*** What other businesses similar to me have achieved with Support Hero software?
- ***Idea:*** Heroes on the Rise: The Support Hero Customer Spotlight

- *Format:* Case Studies showing how Support Hero has produced brands that customers love

BOFU Branded Offer 3

- *What The Prospects Are Searching For (Marketing Triggers):* How Support Hero software will solve my specific problems?
- *Idea:* Product Tour: Top 7 Benefits of Support Hero Software
- *Format:* A virtual product demo/tour of the benefits of the customer support software

RECOMMENDED TOOLS

- For creating virtual product tours: Camtasia[2] for PC, Screenflow for Mac[3]
- For landing page: Hubspot Landing Page Tool,[4] LeadPages,[5] Unbounce[6]

SCOPE OF WORK

- Think of 3 BOFU Branded Content ideas and produce the content
- Out of the 3, create the BOFU content idea that is the easiest to execute
- Create an email campaign to send your branded content to your list
- Identify a call to action and create a landing page where your leads can fulfill that action

METRICS TO TRACK

- # of visits to your lead BOFU content offer landing page
- # of registration for your BOFU content offer such as virtual tours and whitepaper
- % of registration converted to sales opportunity

CHAPTER 12: BOTTOM OF FUNNEL EMAIL NURTURE (SALES CONTENT)

THE 'WHAT' AND THE 'WHY'

Do you remember when you bought your first car?

I do.

I went from one dealership to another until I found one that fit my needs, satisfied my wants, and made sense for my budget.

While car hunting, there was one car that I really fell in love with. A classic convertible. As you may have guessed, the price tag on that beast of a vehicle was a tad bit out of my budget. I loved my first car, but I would have loved the convertible even better.

A few months after purchasing my "second choice," I saw the manager of the dealership where I found that convertible. He asked me if I pushed through with the purchase. I said I did not because of my budget limitations.

"You should have asked me if we can customize a payment plan that works for you. I'm sure we could have come up with something."

"I didn't know that was possible. Dang, I really liked that convertible."

"And we would have loved if you became a client of the dealership."

How is this relevant to the Bottom of Funnel email nurture sequence?

Think about this...

How many prospects would have purchased your products or services if you were able to answer their objections and hesitations? This becomes more important in online marketing since we get limited interaction with our customers compared to businesses with a physical storefront.

In my case, how many additional clients would I have closed if I reached out to them after our first consultation call and asked "Why haven't you signed up yet?" or "What are your biggest hesitations?" In the case of e-commerce merchants, this could be as simple as asking cart abandoners "Why didn't you buy?"

According to eMarketer, email remains to be the best performing channel in terms of converting leads into sales.[1] After giving leads your BOFU Branded Content, you have pretty much weeded out prospects who are not yet ready to buy from warm leads who are ready to purchase.

These leads are now more predisposed to be receptive to your sales messages. This is where the type of content turns a corner from being educational/informative to strategically sell your products and services.

You might be asking: "Why do I need another email nurture sequence at this late stage of my marketing funnel when I've already given my leads a ton of content?" This is because the numbers have proven time and again that having two or more email touchpoints creates more sales as well as encourages repeat purchases.

Messaging is Key

Are you familiar with the saying everyone loves to buy but everyone hates being sold to? When you craft your BOFU email nurture emails, hard-sell, in-your-face sales tactics won't work. While making a sale is your goal, you have to do it through a carefully planned messaging strategy that closes the deal without employing the old-school car salesman tactic.

RECOMMENDED STRATEGY

Based on experience, what I've really found to work for an ever-green Bottom of Funnel email nurture sequence strategy is to use a 5-part email nurture sequence. This formula works best to drum up interest, excitement, and desire for your offer. This also works as an evergreen BOFU email nurture sequence -- you can use the same emails over and over as leads go through your funnel because your messages are not tied to a seasonal promo.

Here's a structure you can follow:

BOFU Email Nurture Sequence

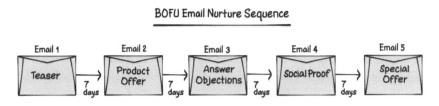

Fig 12.1: 5-part email sequence for bottom of funnel traffic.

Email 1: Teaser

In an article published in Unbounce, Jessica Moon said: "By creating an alluring and irresistible email campaign that teases and builds up anticipation for your project, you can create a great amount of support and succeed in your project goals."[2]

A few days after giving your leads your BOFU Branded Content, send out an email teasing your offer. While they might already have an idea of what it is (assuming that they read your BOFU Branded Content), it's still a great jumpoff point that will also pre-frame them to expect an offer from you in their Inbox.

How To Do It:

- Use a strong hook. Tell a story that will draw them in and make them anticipate your next email. You can harp on an existing pain point that came up during your market research or trigger curiosity with a novelty-oriented message. For example, if you're selling a weight loss product, you can send an email with the following theme: "Gym Instructors Will Lose Clients If This Gets Out".
- Provide enough information to make them feel that whatever you're offering is relevant and useful to them, but leave out enough to keep the anticipation.

Email 2: Product Offer

According to Direct Marketing Association, 66% of consumers have purchased something through email, surpassing the performance of both social media and direct mail.[3] This is the first time that you are pitching your offer to your marketing-qualified leads so this step is crucial in terms of conversions.

How To Do It:

- Your leads will have one question in their head: "What's in it for me?" So, while you're pitching your products/services, make the messages all about them. Use benefit-driven statements. And instead of using "I/We" copy (i.e. "I am offering this product...," "We are excited to announce..."), use "You" copy ("You should take advantage...," "Your next step...").
- The goal of your email is to convince leads to click through to your sales page, not make the sale right there and then. Your leads would need more information before purchasing

and that's too many details to cram into one single email. Sell the click and allow your sales page to close the deal.

- Personalize, personalize, personalize! If you captured their first name when they opted in, use that in your emails. If you can segment your leads based on their needs or using different cohorts, you can tailor fit your messages/copy to match their expectations.

Email 3: Answer Objections

While it's true that you've saturated your leads with your brand messaging at this point, they would still have objections, friction points that will prevent them from making a purchase. This could be your price, after-sales support, or a gap in terms of fully understanding the benefits of your offer to them.

The goal of this email is to answer these objections and to get them over the cliff so to speak.

How To Do It:

- Identify where you can get information regarding frequently asked questions or objections from your previous customers. This could be your sales team, your customer service team, and even your social media team. Compile these questions and make sure that you update them regularly with new questions and objections.
- Don't be defensive. You're not on trial here. You're trying to help your leads take action and make the purchase because it's the most beneficial decision. You can write this email in an FAQ format so it sounds educational and informative.

Email 4: Social Proof

If addressing common objections and answering frequently asked questions don't do the trick, a great strategy is to follow up with an email containing testimonials from your previous and current customers. Social proof can tip the scale when buyers are uncertain whether a product/service is going to work for them.

How To Do It:

- Don't overdo it. Just choose the strongest testimonials that you have. It's ideal if you can find testimonials from customers who were also hesitant to buy at first, to demonstrate that reluctance is just normal.
- Use multimedia if available. "Regular," text testimonials are great, but video testimonials are even better.

Email 5: Special Offer

The reality is even the most sales-qualified leads won't take your offer as is and you need to do more to convert them. As a last tactic in the BOFU email nurture sequence, you can send out a special offer email to encourage trial.

How To Do It:

- Your goal is to minimize the risk for your prospective buyers. A free trial is a great example of this strategy.
- You can also offer free consultations or a one-on-one Q&A session to answer their remaining questions and squash other objections.
- Make sure to manage expectations in terms of succeeding charges or payments. For instance, if you're offering a free trial, be clear when the full price would be in effect.

THE BOFU EMAIL NURTURE SEQUENCE IN ACTION

Below is a sample email autoresponder nurture sequence for the Bottom of Funnel for our imaginary customer support SaaS company **Support Hero**:

Email 1

- **Type:** Teaser
- **Sent on:** Day 1
- **Email Idea:** The World Needs More Support Heroes

Email 2

- **Type:** Product Offer
- **Sent on:** Day 4
- **Email Idea:** Be a Hero to Your Customers Today

Email 3

- **Type:** Answer Objections
- **Sent on:** Day 7
- **Email Idea:** The Most Common Questions We Got

Email 4

- **Type:** Social Proof
- **Sent on:** Day 10
- **Email Idea:** Meet the Heroes Who are Wowing Their Customers

Email 5

- **Type:** Special Offer
- **Sent on:** Day 15
- **Email Idea:** Get Support Hero Risk Free Today!

This is how the BOFU Email Nurture Sequence will look like:

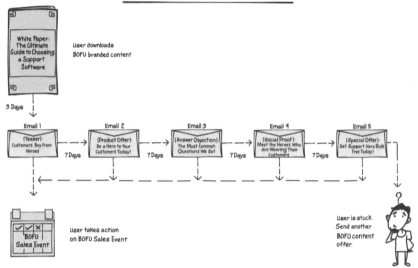

Fig 12.2: Bottom of Funnel email nurture sequence example for Support Hero.

You can download an example of an accomplished BOFU email nurture planning calendar for Support Hero at leadspanda.com/cmb.

FREE RESOURCE: BOFU EMAIL NURTURE SEQUENCE PLANNING TEMPLATE

To help you plan out the content of your BOFU email nurture sequence I have created a template. This planning template is similar to the MOFU nurture sequence planning template that you got from the previous chapter. You can download your free BOFU email nurture planning template at leadspanda.com/cmb.

RECOMMENDED TOOLS

- LeadsPanda BOFU email nurture planning template (Download at leadspanda.com/cmb)
- Email Marketing Tool: MailChimp,[4] Aweber,[5] Infusionsoft[6]

SCOPE OF WORK

- Create a BOFU email flow
- Plan out an email nurture sequence with 5 emails
- Write and execute the 5 emails

METRICS TO TRACK

- Email Open Rate
- Click Through Rate
- Number of sales page views
- Conversion rates from BOFU to a Sales Event

CHAPTER 13: BOTTOM OF FUNNEL SALES EVENT

THE 'WHAT' AND THE 'WHY'

Based on my experience, there are two types of content marketers sitting on the extreme ends of the spectrum when it comes to the Bottom of Funnel Sales Event.

On one end is *Shy Sally*. She is very timid when it comes to selling her products/services to her customers. "If my offers are good enough, customers are going to barge through my shop with very minimal prompting." Shy Sally thinks that selling defeats the purpose of content marketing.

Meanwhile, on the other end is *Hard Sell Heather*. She is a fan of overt sales messages and thinks that the aggressive pitches are the natural final step of content marketing. "If my customers like me and they are ready to buy, they wouldn't mind."

Who do you relate to more? Shy Sally or Hard Sell Heather?"

Finding the Middle Ground

You raised awareness for your brand. You acquired leads, nurtured them, built rapport, and gained their trust. You started shifting your role in their lives from an information provider to a solutions provider with your branded content and your sales-oriented emails.

Finally, it's now time to close the deal.

The Bottom of Funnel Sales Event is the turning point where marketing qualified leads become sales qualified leads and arguably, one of the most crucial stages of the content funnel. If you're a marketer working in a company, this is probably what your C-level executives pay the most attention to because this is where they're going to see actual returns on your content marketing spend.

At this point, your goal becomes single-minded: to make a sale.

Marketing legend Dan Kennedy said: "He who is willing and able to spend the most to acquire customers, wins." The Bottom of Funnel Sales Event puts money in your bank account. It doesn't just mean earnings for you, but a bigger pool to re-invest in your marketing funnels to generate new leads and acquire more customers.

Don't Forget Content

That said, one of the biggest mistakes that marketers make at this stage is what I would like to call "content amnesia." Many become so focused on closing the deal that they revert to hard sell tactics (remember Hard Sell Heather?), which has been proven time and again to not work with today's online consumers. Do this and you're going to waste all the content initiatives you did in the previous funnel steps.

My friend Chris is a Texas-based online entrepreneur who sells courses about web analytics online. I admire Chris when it comes to creating valuable content for his audience. Among the notable ones are two blog posts a week, a free Facebook Live webinar, download-able checklists, and free web analytics reporting templates. Because of his work in this relatively small niche of online marketing, he's been invited to think tanks, masterminds, and marketing confer-ences to share his expertise.

However, despite this arsenal of great content, the take rate on Chris' online course offering is dismal to say the least, hovering at just under 1% conversion rate. His company is able to stay afloat because of the revenue stream from their high-level consultancy clients, but Chris really wants this side of his business to take off because it's more passive, requires less work, and something that he enjoys more.

During one of our Skype conversations, I asked him what content strategy he's implementing at the bottom of his funnel.

"I use a time-tested sales funnel. You know, a sales page with the main offer followed by upsell offers and down-sell offers."

"And in terms of content? How do you confirm sales readiness?," I asked.

"I don't really have a content strategy to confirm sales readiness," Chris admits.

"How do you use content to convert leads into opportunities?," I asked again.

"I just assumed that once I nurture them and they don't opt out, they are ready to buy."

Haven't we all had the same assumption? How wrong were we?

Keep in mind that content is still King at the Bottom of Funnel Sales Event. Yes, your objective changes, but do not overlook the importance of content. In fact, if you deliver high-quality content at your Bottom of Funnel Sales Events, closing the sale would be much easier.

RECOMMENDED STRATEGY

Before we dive into the different ways to deliver content for BOFU Sales Events, here's one golden rule:

Highlight benefits, not features.

Remember, every piece of content that you create - from the top of the funnel to the bottom of the funnel - should be customer-centric. So, as much as you would want to brag about the dozens of amazing features that your products/services include, the focus should be the benefit to buyers. Underscoring the benefits will naturally call attention to the features of your products/services, but in a more conversational and useful tone that will resonate more to your prospects.

Here are the Top 3 Bottom of Funnel Sales Events that have produced the highest conversion rates among businesses cutting across different industries.

1. Webinars

At some point, every marketer or business owner would explore using webinars either to get more leads or customers, but only a handful have succeeded in generating real ROI from them. If you've tried using webinars as a sales strategy in the past but failed, don't give up. Webinars are still one of the highest converting marketing channels, with a take rate ranging from 5% to 20%.[1]

As webinar guru Amy Porterfield said: "Because despite EVERY-THING that can (and usually does) go wrong with a webinar… There is still NOTHING more powerful, leverageable or exponentially more profitable for you and your business than a well-executed webinar strategy."[2]

Here are a few tips on how you can put together high converting and profitable webinars:

1. Not all products should be sold through webinars.
   Typically, putting together a webinar takes time, money, and other resources. That said, low ticket items pitched through webinars won't bring you at break even, let alone give you profit. Ideally, you should sell products/services worth $100 and above during your webinars.
2. Craft an irresistible offer around your product and services.
   It's about how you package and present your offer to your

webinar attendees. Offer discounts, extended warranties, premium support, etc.

3. Give them a reason to take your offer *now*. Scarcity and urgency are two magic words in any successful sales strategy and it's the same with webinars.

4. Provide a replay. Since most webinars are live events, you should anticipate fall out due to availability. This is why you should provide a re-play to those who can't make it live, but are still interested in learning about your offer.

5. Create an email follow-up sequence. Again, webinars could convert between 5% to 20% during your live event. For the remaining 80%-95% of attendees who didn't take your offer on the get-go, create a follow-up email sequence. This sequence will have at least 3 emails following the same format as the BOFU email nurture sequence discussed in the previous chapter.

2. One-On-One Product Demos

Product demos are effective in converting buyers who are still on the fence about whether they should go through the purchase or not. They allow buyers to better visualize how your product/service is going to benefit them.

During your product demos, you don't need to show buyers every benefit of your products/services. According to product demo expert and author of the book *Just F*cking Demo* Rob Falcone: "You need to show your prospects only the specific features that they need to achieve what they want so that you can get the result you're aiming for. The success of a demo depends on your prospects understanding the value you could add."[3]

Here are 5 things to keep in mind when giving product demos:

1. Please, don't do a cookie-cutter demo for all buyers. When buyers set an appointment with you for a live online product demo, get to know their circumstances better. Using this information, prepare a product demo that is

customized to their specific scenarios, problems, and needs.

2. Demo your product in the specific context of the buyer. Don't just read a script or do an oration of your product's features. Tell a story. Use verbal cues that will connect with buyers.
3. Practice, practice, practice. Remember, every demo is different so always prepare beforehand.
4. There's nothing more disastrous than going through a product demo to find out that there's something broken or something's not working. Make sure to test everything before your live demo.
5. Close the sale. Be direct and straightforward in communicating what the next step is.

3. Free Consultations/Assessments

Many times, buyers don't push through with their purchase because they are not sure whether your offer is right for them. This is where free consultations and assessments come in.

With free one-on-one consultations, you are able to evaluate how a specific buyer fares against the description of your ideal customer avatar and advise him whether to go ahead and proceed with the purchase or offer another product or service.

It is extremely important that you give honest assessments. If your offer doesn't meet the requirements of your buyers, inform them. Forcing buyers to continue with their purchase even if you know that your offer is incompatible to their needs will lead to high product returns and bad reviews for your brand.

An important note about offering free consultations and assessments: Know when to stop. Consultations and assessments are like a good movie trailer. You want to just show enough to get the audience interested and actually watch the film once it premieres.

A SEAMLESS TRANSITION FROM CONTENT MARKETING TO SALES GENERATION

After extensive content marketing, your sales team should be ready to deal with sales-qualified leads that seamlessly ties into the content marketing strategy that you employed. A sales qualified lead (SQL) is a prospect created by the marketing department and vetted by the sales team. After initial contact from marketing, your sales team should deal with sales-qualified leads in the context that these leads are ready to buy your products and services.

For a seamless transition, you can follow the sales process below:

1. Confirm Sales Readiness

Your sales team should be able to identify how ready your leads are to make a purchase by asking the following questions:

- Do they have clarifications about your product?
- Do they understand how your products/services can benefit them?
- Are they considering other options or solution providers?

At this stage, your sales team should have solid content to address any objections and clarifications that your leads might have.

2. Upgrade the Lead to an Opportunity

If the lead is well-informed about what they need, and actively considering your products and services, your sales team must label them as an opportunity. At this point, the lead is truly primed to consume your bottom of funnel offer. The next step for your team is to send a proposal for products or services. The efficiency of your sales team should be evaluated based on the number of opportunities that are actually converting into paying customers.

3. Track the Revenue Back to the Source

An old marketing adage reminds us time and again: "You can't manage what you cannot measure." If you follow everything in this content marketing framework, you will be able to attribute sales to specific content marketing initiatives, and therefore give you insightful data on what's working and what's not.

RECOMMENDED TOOLS

- For webinars: WebinarJam,[4] GoToWebinar[5]
- For one-on-one meetings: UberConference,[6] GoToMeeting,[7] Skype[8]

SCOPE OF WORK

- Create a Bottom of Funnel Sales Offer
- Create a Landing Page with Your Sales Offer
- Include the offer in your BOFU Follow Up Email

METRICS TO TRACK

- # of Sales Qualified Leads
- # of Opportunities
- Pageviews to your Sales Page
- Sales Page to Purchase Conversion Rate
- Cart Abandonment Rate

CHAPTER 14: SOCIAL MEDIA POSTINGS & PROMOTIONS

THE 'WHAT' AND THE 'WHY'

I n his book *Jab, Jab, Jab, Right Hook*, Gary Vaynerchuk perfectly described how social media has become an intrusive and invasive force in the everyday lives of people:

"Where's your phone?

In your back pocket? On the table in front of you? In your hands because you're using it to read this book? It's probably somewhere within easy reach, unless you're one of those people who are constantly misplacing their phones and my question has you rummaging through the laundry basket again or checking under your car seat. If you're in a public space, look around. I mean it, pop your head up. What do you see? Phones. Some people are doing the old-fashioned thing and using them to actually talk to another person. But I predict that someone, and probably several someones, within a four-foot radius is playing Dots. Or double-tapping a picture. Or composing a status update. Or sharing a picture. Or tweeting. In fact, unless you're visiting Aunt Sally in the nursing home—and even then, you'd be surprised at how iPads are crashing the ninety-year old demo lately—it's more than likely that almost everyone around you has a smartphone in his or her possession, and if not a phone, then a tablet. I know this because there are nearly 325 million mobile subscriptions in the United States alone.

And when people are using their devices, it's probable that almost half are networking on social media."[1]

In 2004, Facebook started an online phenomenon that changed how people communicate, consume online content, and search for products and services. There were other social media networks that came before Facebook, but it's undeniable that this Mark Zuckerberg creation paved the way for something else. Of course, the rest is history as more social platforms such as Twitter, LinkedIn, Instagram, and Pinterest rose to popularity as well.

It was not a surprise that social media has also changed how businesses marketed their products and services.

It's quite simple: if you don't have a social media presence, you are invisible to billions of buyers worldwide who, according to recent statistics, spend more than 2 hours 15 minutes per day browsing through social media content.[2] There are case studies after case studies of how businesses are able to use social networks to grow their businesses. So, there's not a shadow of a doubt whether social media can deliver results.

It's a matter of employing the right strategies and tactics to get the results that you want.

The Two-Pronged Goal of Social Media Postings and Promotions

Social media can fulfill different business needs, but in this Content Marketing Blueprint, I am concerned with two primary objectives:

1. Driving traffic to your website
2. Generating referrals from your current customers

The first one is quite obvious. As mentioned, more than 3 billion people are currently on social media and it's growing by 13% yearly.[3] The task for business owners then becomes capturing users who belong to their customer avatars from these billions.

The second goal is closely connected to your Bottom of Funnel strategy. After converting leads into customers, your goal now is to convert these buyers into your brand ambassadors - generating word of mouth for your brand and driving referral customers for your business.

RECOMMENDED STRATEGY

Traffic-Generating Tactics

As mentioned, not all social media traffic is created equal. Social media users are diverse - they come from all walks of life with different buying motivations. Your goal is to capture people who fit your customer avatars using social media content that will bring them to your website and turn them into leads.

How do you turn your social media assets into traffic generating machines for your business?

1. Follow Ground Rules on Timing, Frequency, and Content-to-Promo Ratio

While you can approach social media content marketing in several ways, there are certain rules based on time-tested data that you should follow.

- **Timing**. While people are hooked on social media all day, every day, based on research, there are certain times during the day that get the most engagement.[4] For example, on Facebook, the best time to post is between 12 pm and 3 pm on weekdays, and between 12 pm and 1 pm on weekends. If you use a social media automation software such as Buffer and Hootsuite, you can view a report showing you which times your content is getting the most engagement and you can adjust accordingly.

- **Frequency**. Everyone hates spammers. As a general rule, don't post more than twice a day, unless you're a publication such as BuzzFeed. Hubspot found out that sharing more than the recommended frequency per day significantly reduces the level of engagement.[5]
- **Content-to-Promo Ratio**. As with any other content channel, your social media posts should first and foremost provide value. Don't overload your social media channels with product promotions. To be on the safe side, follow the 2:1 rule - ⅓ of your social media posts should be about you, your product and your own content; ⅔ should be curated content from other sources.

Just to reiterate, your social media content should include posts that promote your products and services directly. I see a lot of marketers who are afraid to do this, fearing that their followers may find it too hard sell. As long as you still provide valuable, entertaining, useful and relevant content, there is no problem if you promote your offers via social media.

2. Choose the Right Social Media Channel

Not all content shared on Facebook will be as effective in generating traffic when shared on LinkedIn and vice versa. Every social network creates different user experiences and your content should be tailor fitted to each channel.

Granted that there would be some overlap, but customize your content as much as possible.

Here's a general guideline on what content would work best on each channel:

- Facebook: Curated content, your blog posts, videos, live streams via Facebook Live

- Twitter: Breaking news, curated content, shoutouts to industry influencers
- LinkedIn: Company news, thought leadership content, industry updates, job openings
- Instagram: Owned photos, crowdsourced images, quotes, short videos via Instagram stories
- Pinterest: Infographics, step-by-step image guides

3. Your Ultimate Goal: Virality

Believe it or not, but many of the posts that go viral involve cats. People on social media just can't seem to get enough of feline cuties. I don't know about you, but when I see cute cat videos, memes, or photos on my social feed, I can't help myself but to take a second look.

Who better to capitalize on this craze than the biggest kitten and senior cat food brand in the world, Whiskas. Through its partner agencies, Whiskas created a series of videos it called Kitten College. According to a Whiskas representative: "We wanted to not only reach their brains, but reach their hearts."[6]

The videos generated more than 39 million views and increased Whiskas' brand recall by 47%. Imagine if you could do the same for your brand.

If you want to get a significant amount of traffic from social media, you can't do it alone. You need the help of your followers and other social media users to share your content on their own feeds. The success of many social media superstar brands such as BuzzFeed is the virality of the content that they create.

- Use videos and images. Visual content gets more shares.
- Create an emotional hook. People will share content that makes them laugh, cry, or think deeply about a topic they care about.
- Create useful content. People would share content on their

own social media feeds if they think it will help their friends and peers. This is why listicles are effective.

Virality also applies to your promotional content. For example, if you want people to download something from your website, you can ask them to first take a quiz and the downloadable content that they will get is going to be based on their answers to the quiz.

4. Create an Open Loop

If you're sharing your own content such as your blog posts, create an open loop - give just the right amount of information to intrigue people and prompt them to click on your site to get more.

You can post an interesting snippet from your blog or post questions to drum up interest.

5. Tap Into the Social Media Capital of Influencers in Your Industry

Social media users will click on and share content that is credible. The best way to generate credibility for your social media content is getting social media influencers to share them. Just take a look at Oprah. Different people from different fields such as Suze Orman and Dr. Oz have skyrocketed to popularity because Oprah featured them on her show.

In short:

You, talking about yourself = not very impactful

Credible, well-known people talking about you = very powerful

How do you get social media influencers to share your content:

- **Share their content**. One of the best ways for influencers to notice you is if you share their content. Say something positive and how it has helped you. Be sure to tag them so they get alerted.

- **Comment on their blogs**. Really engage them in a dialogue and have meaningful conversations with them. There have been many instances when influencers took notice of people leaving valuable comments on their blogs which paved the way to a rewarding professional relationship.
- **Ask them if you could contribute content for their blog**. Many industry publications do accept guest blog posts so make sure you create a list of these sites and start reaching out to them.
- **Create high-value content on your own site**. Credible people will only share content from trustworthy resources. There is no way that social media influencers would want to share your content if it is poorly executed and won't really add value to their own followers.
- **Consider giving their followers a special deal on your offers**. Influencers will be more inclined to promote your products or services if you offer an exclusive deal for their followers. In return for the word-of-mouth and traffic that you will be getting, you are helping them create goodwill for their followers.

Referral Generating Tactics

At the bottom of the funnel, content doesn't stop working once you have closed the deal. Many businesses miss out on generating more sales by generating referral customers using social media content.

1. Ask for Social Media Testimonials

According to Nielsen's Trust in Advertising Report, 84% of buyers on social media consider their family and friends as their trusted sources when it comes to shopping online.[7] Many social media users will crowdsource opinions from their social media friends and connections if they are uncertain whether to go through with a purchase or not.

Personally, I am walking and living proof that social media testimonials work wonders when it comes to influencing people's buying decisions. Right now, I rarely purchase anything without searching for reviews on social media. Whether I'm looking for a new restaurant, booking a hotel room, and even when searching for online courses and marketing conferences to learn something new.

Here's something ironic. People are not as predisposed to writing good reviews on social media as they are to sharing negative reviews. In short, buyers will almost always rant on social media if they have a bad experience with a brand, but it will take more prompting for them to spread positive word-of-mouth.

You should have a follow-up strategy to ask social media reviews from your customers. Give them ample time to use and benefit from your products and services, then reach out to them for a testimonial. For an added motivation, offer incentives such as a discount on their next purchase.

2. Turn Them Into Your Affiliates

A lot of e-commerce sites have been turning their customers into their affiliates. Instead of giving out commissions, they give their customers a promo code that their friends and family can use. The system detects when their promo code is used and it earns them credit that they can apply on their succeeding purchases.

As a result, you see many online shoppers today posting positive reviews of products they purchased online, and encouraging their friends to buy using their promo code. It's a good strategy that you can apply for your own business.

3. Encourage Sharing Right After Purchase

While time is needed for your customers to write full reviews of your products and services, you can encourage them to share something general about their recent purchase with you on social media.

The best way to do this is by having a social sharing widget on your order confirmation page. Provide a pre-written post for them so all they need to do is to click on a button and they're done. Some pre-written post ideas are:

- "Proud new owner of..."
- "Taking (name of your product or service) for a spin..."
- "Decided to take a step toward (a goal of your customers that your product fulfills i.e. losing weight)..."

This allows you to get immediate referral prospects from your most recent customers.

4. Feature Success Stories on Your Page

Once you get testimonials flowing in, you will start seeing who among your customers you've dramatically helped through your products and services. What you can do is to reach out to them and tell them that you're going to feature them on your social media pages.

The next step is to get to know them better, ask how your products helped them and build a more compelling story. It would be better if you have supporting visuals such as a recorded video interview.

Remember what we said about positioning your customers as the heroes of your content? This is one of the best ways to do it. You're featuring how they achieved success and by doing so, it creates a positive halo effect on your products.

Once you post the content on your social media pages, don't forget to tag them. This will give them something to brag about and share your post on their own social media accounts. If the story is compelling enough, there's a good chance that their social media friends and contacts will take an interest in your products.

5. Use Exclusivity

Remember the time when Gmail was by invitation only? Everyone was desperate to get their own Gmail account and many went the distance just to get in. And those who had the power to invite weren't too shy to brag about it.

You can do the same with social media referrals. Give your current customers the power to invite their social media contacts into something that is exclusive - whether to a closed Facebook group that you have or a private webinar that you are hosting. It's a great way to leverage your current customers to create word-of-mouth for your brand.

FREE RESOURCE: SOCIAL MEDIA CALENDAR TEMPLATE

As with any other form of content, organization, tracking, and scheduling are extremely important for social media postings.

I have created a handy social media calendar to organize your social media posts that you and the rest of your entire team can easily use. Download your free social media calendar template online at leadspanda.com/cmb.

RECOMMENDED TOOLS

- LeadsPanda Social Media Calendar Template (Download at leadspanda.com/cmb)
- For social media postings: Buffer,[8] Hootsuite,[9] Edgar[10]

SCOPE OF WORK

- Create 14 social media posts, good for one week (2x posts per day)
- Use the social media calendar template
- Use Buffer to schedule the posts

METRICS TO TRACK

- # of page likes
- # of people reached by a post
- Engagement (# of Likes, Comments, etc.)
- # of link clicks to website

CHAPTER 15: GUEST POSTING

THE 'WHAT' AND THE 'WHY'

N*o content marketer is an island.*

All the best content marketers know that they cannot do it alone and now, you are in on the secret. Why do you think everyone is striving to become viral? Or why social media has become a part of the core of any digital marketing strategy? Or why do you think user-generated content continues to thrive?

It's because content is a crucial element in your inbound marketing and you need external channels to get more traffic and convert this traffic into conversion opportunities.

Leveraging Other People's Popularity and Network

In the U.S., when people need life advice, one of the names they turn to is Dr. Phil. While Rachel Ray is someone home cooks refer to when they need a new recipe.

They are practically celebrities in their own right.

So, what catapulted them to their current well-regarded celebrity status? If you answered their talents and expertise, you're right, but that's not the secret sauce.

It was Oprah.

Even Dr. Phil attributes his success to Oprah. "When you get into Oprah's orbit it doesn't affect your career, it defines your career," said Dr. Phil. "I had no desire to be on television before and she made me see the value of it and she made me understand the power of it and without Oprah there would be no 'Dr. Phil.' That's a pretty big impact."

The positive impact that Oprah has in launching people's careers and businesses is so powerful that it actually has a name: *The Oprah Effect.*

Guest blogging mimics this halo effect which is why I particularly like it as a content marketing strategy.

Before downloading this book, you probably haven't heard my name or who I am. Alas, you're already reading Chapter 15 of this book and could still be clueless why you should listen to anything I'm saying here (but if you made it this far, you probably know already).

On the other hand, let's say this book was referenced by digital marketing titans such as Neil Patel, Ryan Deiss, or Rand Fishkin. Would that make me instantly credible in your eyes? I bet it would.

At its very core, guest posting is about piggybacking on the influence of more established names in your industry by providing them with great content in exchange for access to their network.

Proving that Guest Posting Works: Buffer's 100,000 Signups Plus More Success Stories

Who doesn't know Buffer? It's now a household name among content marketers and one of the most common tools in every business owner's content marketing arsenal.

Buffer co-founder Leo Widrich recalled how Buffer rose to success with guest blogging at the core of its content marketing strategy.

"Solely through guest blogging we've acquired around 100,000 users within the first 9 months of running Buffer. It's been something that was very gradual though. Within the space of around 9 months, I wrote around 150 guest posts. Of course the early ones barely drove any traffic and only very gradually did things improve, I think that's very important to understand. It will take a while until you can find the right frequency of posting."

When asked how much time he spent writing guest posts, he replied: "All of my time! Frankly, when content marketing was our full focus, that's all I did. Two to four articles every day, nothing else. Sitting down, hammering out great content, getting it featured as guest posts, doing the same in the morning again."[1]

This addresses one of the biggest guest blogging blocks marketers and business owners face -- the amount of time and effort that is required to produce engaging content. If you're challenged by the same thing, know that the rewards waiting, in the end, are worth it.

Here are success stories to get you inspired:

- Gregory Ciotti of HelpScout was able to generate almost 37,000 new email subscribers from guest blogging[2]
- Through a guest post in Moz, Point Blank SEO was able to generate 400 new visitors and acquire 2 new clients[3]
- A single guest post written by Bryan Harris of Videofruit.com for OkDork.com jumpstarted the success of his business which is now earning $15,000 per month[4]

Their success stories are just the tip of the iceberg. There are many more businesses out there that are reaping the benefits of guest posting as you're reading is.

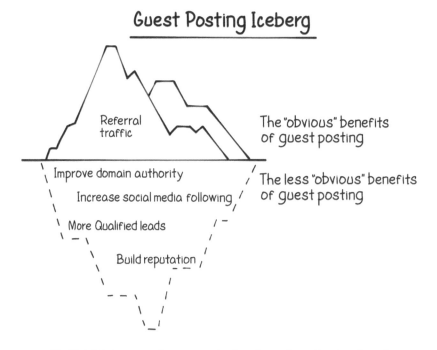

Fig 15.1: Marketers see the guest posting benefits on the surface, but the real benefits come in ways they can't see.

Speaking of seeing just the tip of the iceberg, the additional traffic that you will be getting with guest posting is just the tip of the iceberg because there are a ton more benefits to guest blogging than meets the eye. These benefits include:

1. Increase your domain authority. Guest blogging allows you to acquire backlinks coming from high authority sites. In turn, this boosts the domain authority of your own site, which is a known ranking factor in Google's algorithm. According to HubSpot's Clifford Chi: "From Google's perspective, domain authority is like your website's reputation as a thought leader. The search engine uses your domain authority to make sure you can provide the highest-quality content about your specific subject matter. If you do, you'll have good domain authority and Google will boost your content's rankings. If you don't, you'll have bad domain authority and they won't rank your content."[5]

2. Grow your social media following. Popular sites promote their new blog posts via their social media assets. This is good news for you because this means that you will get additional exposure in social media. Sometimes, the sites you create guest posts for will even give you a shoutout and tag you in their social media posts, which is an added bonus because people on social media can checkout your profile and connect directly with you.

3. Get more qualified leads. People who follow certain sites and influencers are often more engaged. Guest blogging allows you to connect with them, get them over to your website, and turn them into leads. While they will go through the same nurture sequence as your other leads, there's a higher chance that you will convert these leads into opportunities.

4. Improve your authority and reputation. Aside from strengthening the domain authority of your website, guest blogging also fortifies your authority as an expert in your field. For instance, if I'm browsing Copyblogger and I see John Doe's post there, I would think that John Doe has to have a high level of expertise in copy-writing for him to be invited to write for a reputable site such as Copyblogger.

RECOMMENDED STRATEGY

Honestly, right at this very moment, you can just identify a website that accepts guest blogs, pitch a topic, and run away with it. However, just like any other worthy content marketing endeavor, guest posting requires a structure.

To start you on the right track, here's a 10-step guest posting strategy. Borrowing from one of Disney's classic fairy tales Beauty and the Beast, just remember the phrase B.E. O.U.R. G.U.E.S.T. as a mnemonic for this 10-step strategy:

B IS FOR BUILD CLEAR AND SPECIFIC OBJECTIVES

Just to reiterate: no content should be made for content's sake. That said, every guest post you write should be in line with clear and specific goals. The top 5 common goals for guest posting are:

1. Drive traffic to a landing page, to your blog, or other pages in your site to generate more leads and sales
2. Build awareness for your brand
3. Get more SEO juice for your site by increasing the number of your inbound links
4. Position yourself as an authority to increase speaking engagements and other opportunities
5. Generate more email subscribers or social media followers

It's important to have clear objectives so you can tailor fit the content of your guest posts. These goals will also determine which page/pages on your site, your guest post will link to.

E IS FOR EXPLORE ALL POSSIBLE GUEST BLOGGING OPPORTUNITIES

Once you know your goals, the next step is to find sites that accept guest posts.

There are 2 methods to doing this that I find effective, and they're not that difficult to do:

Method 1. Do A Google Search. You can use several queries to generate a list of sites that are accepting guest posts. These include:

- Keyword/topic/industry + "guest blog"
- Keyword/topic/industry + "write for us"
- Keyword/topic/industry + "guest post"

You can find more queries at optimizesmart.com.[6]

Method 2. Search on Twitter. An alternative to Google is Twitter. You can use the same queries above and you will see authors

Tweeting about their guest posts or the websites themselves sharing the content.

When looking for guest blogging opportunities, do it in such a way that you are building a laundry list. Having said this, you should not just look to sites within your immediate niche or industry. In order to build a robust list, you should employ a tactic called *market overlap*.

A concept coined by Authority Hacker, market overlap is a technique that explores guest blogging topics where your niche overlaps another niche.[7] For instance, if I were building a guest blogging laundry list for LeadsPanda, aside from the content marketing niche, I will also explore sites in the following industries:

- Ecommerce
- SEO
- Entrepreneurship
- Web design and development
- Social media marketing

These are the obvious industries closely related to content marketing. However, you can virtually submit a guest blog to any site in any niche as long as you can create topics that lies in the common ground between the two niches. For instance, below is an example of how you can create a topic for building and construction blog:

Market Overlap

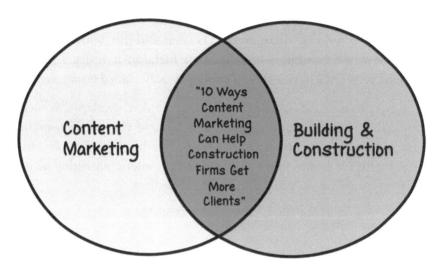

Fig 15.2: Market overlap technique to find guest posting opportunity in any industry.

Of course, it's up to the sites if they will accept your guest post or not, but at this stage, the more authoritative guest blogging sites you can find, the better.

O IS FOR OPPORTUNITIES ASSESSMENT

Your initial list should be a laundry list because you're going to scrub out some of the sites you found because they are not a good fit for your brand, your content, and what you're trying to achieve with guest posting.

Below are some of the criteria that you should use when evaluating websites for guest blogging:

Audience. At this point, you should already have a strong grasp of your content avatars. You should know who your ideal target readers are. Even if a website publishes content that is related to your business, their audience may not be in sync with yours. For example, if you're writing about content marketing for advanced marketers, you cannot write for a website that publishes about content marketing for beginners.

Domain Authority. Domain authority is a rating that determines the potential of a domain to rank high in search. Obviously, you would want to submit guest posts to sites with relatively high domain authority. Moz has a free tool called the Link Explorer that you can use to do this.

Another important reason why you would want to submit guest posts to sites with a high domain authority is because you want to be on the good side of Google. As you may already know, Google did a crackdown on spammy content over the course of many years by rolling out several algorithm updates. If you have a link leading back to your site on a site that Google deems as spammy, you might get penalized for it. Submitting guest posts to high authority sites is to err on the side of caution.

Size of Social Media Following. When websites publish a new blog post, whether it's written by one of their own authors or a guest contributor, they will likely promote it on their social media accounts. Of course, the more following the have, the more mileage your content is going to get.

Aside from the criteria above, you can also check for other credibility indicators. For example, check for any sort of engagement between the site and key influencers in your industry, etc.

U IS FOR UNDERSTAND THE SITES' GUEST POSTING GUIDELINES

While one of the objectives of websites that accept guest posting is to diversify their content and offer different perspectives, they still want to maintain certain standards to make. They often provide guidelines that you need to know thoroughly before pitching your guest post idea. These guidelines often include:

- Required length of the post

- Point of view (first, second, or third person)
- Content sensitivities (i.e. any reference to religious or political issues)
- Allowed external links
- Editing policies
- Other requirements such as a Gravatar

Violate these requirements and you risk offending the site owners and ruining any chance for partnership with them.

Once you understand the guest posting requirements, it's time to do your due diligence and research for a blog topic that you can pitch — not just any topic, but a winning topic. A topic that the site owners wish they could have thought on their own. Make sure the topic you choose is "hot" and current. If you have proprietary data or use case studies/anecdotes that you can share, make sure you indicate it.

R IS FOR RECORD EVERYTHING IN A GUEST POSTING CONTENT CALENDAR

Similar to maintaining a content calendar for posts you publish on your own blog, you need to have a content calendar for guest posting. This is to ensure that your guest posts are properly spaced out. It also serves as a detailed project tracker of all your guest blogging initiatives. You can download the guest posting calendar template at leadspanda.com/cmb.

G IS FOR GET YOUR BEST PITCH READY

Finally, the all-important pitch. When it comes to pitches, you need to keep it as concise as possible. Sites that accept guest posts, especially popular ones, get a lot of proposals daily. Your pitch should be clear, to the point, and easy to read. Below are the elements that should be included In your pitch:

- The working headline/topic of your post
- 3 short bullet points on what the post is about

- The benefits of the post to their readers
- Why you're the best person to write the post

U IS FOR UNIQUE CONTENT FOR THE SITES' READERS

It may take a few days before you hear back from a site owner regarding your pitch. Also, you may need to do a couple of follow ups to give them a gentle nudge.

Once your pitch is accepted, it's time to write the actual content of your guest post. Writing a killer guest post is no different than writing a blog post for your own site (so you can revisit the R.E.S.U.L.T.S. Framework), except for one thing. You need to create content that is unique to the site's readers. Take time to really get to know what the readers want in terms of information and writing style. Tailor fit your content to make the site owners feel that you took the time to put together a custom content for their readers.

E IS FOR ENGAGEMENT MONITORING

Congratulations, your guest post has been approved and has been published. However, your work is not over yet. Within the first few hours after your guest post goes live, make sure that you are constantly tracking engagement. Respond to questions promptly and offer any additional information to help readers understand the post better. This also solidifies that you're an expert on the subject.

S IS FOR START TRACKING RESULTS

Make sure that you are monitoring traffic coming from your guest posts and if it's driving other positive business results such as increasing your number of leads and sales.

T IS FOR TARGET LONG-TERM PARTNERSHIPS

Guest posting is not a one-off initiative. Once you become a guest contributor to these publications, you need to maintain a strong partnership with them. This will allow you to submit more guests posts in the future. You may also be tapped as a regular contributor. This will enable you to get consistent traffic from your guest posts.

To summarize the 10-step strategy:

Build Clear and Specific Objectives

Explore All Possible Guest Blogging Opportunities

Opportunities Assessment

Understand the Sites' Guest Posting Guidelines

Record Everything in a Guest Posting Content Calendar

Get Your Best Pitch Ready

Unique Content for the Sites' Readers

Engagement Monitoring

Start Tracking Results

Target Long-Term Partnerships

Now, let's take a closer look at the guest posting content calendar.

FREE RESOURCE: GUEST POSTING CALENDAR TEMPLATE

To help you get started with guest posting right away, I have created a guest posting calendar template. Download your free guest posting calendar template at leadspanda.com/cmb.

RECOMMENDED TOOLS

- LeadsPanda guest posting calendar template (Download at leadspanda.com/cmb)
- Moz for domain authority (DA)[8], Ahrefs for domain rating (DR)[9]

SCOPE OF WORK

- Find 5 websites/publications that are accepting blog posts
- Come up with topics for these websites
- Create a Gravatar profile
- Plot your topics on the LeadsPanda Guest Posting Calendar
- Prepare your initial pitches

METRICS TO TRACK

- # of social shares on published guest posts
- # of comments on published guest posts
- Referral traffic from guest posts

CHAPTER 16: FORUM MARKETING

THE 'WHAT' AND THE 'WHY'

W atching how content marketing and search engine optimization evolves really fascinates me.

I'm not sure if you also noticed, but one of the recent developments that caught my attention is how forum content is starting to show up on the first page of Google's SERPs. For instance, a search on "best ways to do content marketing" will show a thread from Quora at the seventh spot on Google's first page.

I believe forum content is going to be more visible in SERPs, which is why we started doing forum marketing for ourselves and our clients.

Still at its infancy stage, forum marketing is an overlooked gem of content marketing. There are very few content marketers who include a forum marketing strategy in their overall content marketing machine. However, those who do, reap great rewards.

Content marketing expert Tim Ohlrich thinks that marketers who are not using forums are wasting a big opportunity: "One of the biggest mistakes I see in content marketing campaigns is limiting content to your site. Forums are a perfect place to write short-form content that helps your customers. I was in a small business forum recently where someone had asked a question a few days earlier about how to build an online marketing plan. I made a comment about how analyzing backlinks to similar companies can be a great way to figure out what options are out there, and then pointed to a blog post I wrote on the subject a few months back. I don't care if that link is nofollowed. I answered that person's question and had the ability to drive referral traffic to our site. That is a "win" in my book."[1]

According to Pew Research, 15% of all internet users use online forums.[2] With over 3.5 billion internet users, that would mean there are more than 525 million active users on these forums. Among the biggest online forums and discussion boards, Quora reports that it gets 300 million monthly active users while Reddit has 330 million active users, surpassing that of Twitter. Reddit is also the 6th most visited website in the world.[3][4]

The same Pew Research also reveals that 80% of those who are using online forums are earning between $30,000 to upwards of $75,000. This means that forum users range from customers who have some purchasing power to buyers with really high purchasing power.

So, while it is true that your content marketing will survive (and will probably thrive) without a forum content marketing strategy, tapping into this often neglected channel can earn your business unexplored opportunities for traffic, leads, and sales.

Why Invest Time in Forum Marketing?

Have you ever heard of the saying that *customers who ask questions are the best customers?*

This is because well-informed buyers are better customers. They invest time and effort in defining what their needs and problems are and spending a lot of thought comparing solution providers. If you're targeting this specific customer psychographic, online forum users are some of the most well-informed customers on the planet.

In terms of how online forums influence buying decisions, according to a research: "The 'searchable content' within online forums provides a strong indication that forums are influential during the information search, evaluation, purchase and post-purchase stages of the decision making process. Consumers are turning to online forums in order to share knowledge, which in turn, influences their purchase decisions."[5] Of those who were surveyed, 77% agree that the information they read on online forums affects their purchase decisions. Among them, 75% said they will buy products that get positive discussions while 68% said they will not buy products that get negative discussions.

Forum Threads Can Go Viral

Surprised? Don't be. Today, virality is not only a marketing concept confined to social media. I've seen several reddit posts that have gone viral.

As an example, let me retell the story of Reddit Marketing expert and founder of Ghost Influence Brian Swichkow.

So, what did Brian do? Brian got his feet at viral marketing in 2013 when he decided to prank his roommate with targeted Facebook ads. Brian's friend would open his Facebook account and every day for 3 weeks, he would see intimate details about himself on his feed. As a finale to his grand scheme, Brian ran an ad that said "Ever feel like your roommate is creating Facebook ads targeted to a niche of just you?"

He documented what he did and shared it on Reddit. In just 72 hours, his Reddit post generated 450,000 views.

I can only imagine what 450,000 views that could also translate to 450,000 clicks and new visitors to my website could do for my business. It's an unexplored well of traffic that can drive an unimaginable slew of traffic if you know the formula to great forum content marketing.

RECOMMENDED STRATEGY

Now that you know that business case for including forum marketing in your overall content marketing strategy, here is a simple framework I call '**The 5 C forum formula**' that you can implement to make forum marketing help you get more traffic, new leads, and higher sales:

1. Choose which Forums You're Going to be Active In

There are hundreds of online forums out there and the reality is you cannot be present in all of them even if you want to. For starters, you can establish a presence in the communities with the biggest following and feature members with diverse interests such as Quora and Reddit. Then you can research for niche forums that are specific to your industry with the most active and biggest audience.

Brian Swichkow shares this tip about selecting a community or forum to participate in: "The key is to better understand what communities deem to be of value and how you can be the one to create or deliver that to them. It's a bit like language immersion. By breaking down the structure of the platform and the psychology of the message in an accessible manner you will quickly become fluent."[6]

2. Create a Credibility-Optimized Profile

One question or thread in online forums can generate hundreds even thousands of responses. Why should the forum members trust yours?

The first step in gaining the community's trust is writing a well thought out profile when you sign up. When they click on your profile link, members will be asking who you are and what makes you one of the best persons to provide answers to their questions. If you're using Quora, this is even more important because Quora displays the first 50 characters of your bio beside your username when you answer questions.

Here are some of the most basic things you need to include in your profile:

- An appropriate image
- Detailed About Me section
- Your areas of expertise and interests
- The company and other organizations you're affiliated with
- Links to your social media accounts (just make sure your social accounts are updated and feature great content)

3. Choose Relevant Topics and Setup Notifications for Them

Online forums make it really easy for its users to find relevant topics and threads with an easy-to-use search functionality. Just use the search bar and you can find a list of related topics. Select those that are the most relevant to your brand/business. Also, look at other things such as upvotes to make sure that you are following those that are the most active. Then you can set up a notification that allows you to receive an email every time there's a new activity on the thread/question.

4. Choose the Questions You Will Answer and Include Them in Your Content Calendar

You cannot possibly answer all questions in online forums, so you need to be really strategic in choosing. As a general guideline, ask yourself the following questions during your selection process:

- Is this question/thread getting a lot of attention?
- Does this question touch on a trending/hot topic in my industry?
- Will answering this question demonstrate my expertise?
- Does answering this question have the potential to drive traffic to my site and get me more leads?
- Can I answer this question with authority?

Once you've identified the questions you're going to answer, make sure that you plot them in your content calendar just to make sure that it gets done, especially if there are multiple members in your team who will help you craft your responses. However, unlike an editorial calendar for blog posts which has longer lead times, writing answers to forum questions should be treated with much urgency and should be considered time sensitive. This is to ensure your answer is still relevant by the time you post it.

5. Create & Submit Authentic Answers

Write your answers as if you're writing a short-form blog post, around 500-600 words. Answers should be well-written, free of grammatical errors, and should contain useful and actionable insights. Other things that will add authority to your answers include:

- Statistics
- Proprietary data/commissioned research
- Case studies/personal anecdotes

You can also include a link to one of your blog posts in your answers, as long as it's relevant and provides users to get more in-depth content. Do not do it in such a way that it's obvious that you are just trying to get more traffic to your site.

Forum marketing may not be considered a must-have by content marketers, but if you do it well, it gives you access to some of the most informed buyers out there. This gives you an opportunity to build relationships with them, gain their trust, and hopefully, get more leads and customers.

FREE RESOURCE: QUORA MARKETING CALENDAR TEMPLATE

You can create a forum marketing calendar, depending on which forum you are posting and what's going to work best for your company. However, I do recommend that you use my quora marketing calendar template. It's simple and easy, and you can quickly customize it for other forums too. Download your free quora marketing calendar template online at leadspanda.com/cmb.

RECOMMENDED TOOLS

- LeadsPanda Quora marketing calendar template (Download at leadspanda.com/cmb)
- Quora,[7] Reddit[8]

SCOPE OF WORK

- Identify which forums you want to participate in and create a profile in those forums
- Look for relevant topics/threads and set up email notification
- Choose 3 questions you can answer authoritatively

METRICS TO TRACK

- # of like/upvotes for your answers
- Traffic coming from links in your answers

CHAPTER 17: PAID PROMOTIONS

THE 'WHAT' AND THE 'WHY'

The Wright Brothers were not the only ones attempting to build the world's first successful airplane when they did in 1903. There were many who came before them who tried and failed. There were also several inventors who were building similar aircraft at the same time that the Wright Brothers invented the "Flyer."

So, what did the Wright Brothers do that the others didn't?

During that time, aviation engineers were too focused on building powerful engines. Taking a different approach, the Wright Brothers focused on solving a basic problem that they thought plagued the failed experiments that came before them — control. So, instead of focusing on creating powerful engines, they focused on the airplane itself, the structure, the aerodynamics.

The basics.

They added the engines later on.

Fig 17.1: Fix your content marketing funnel (plane) before spending money on ads (engine).

The same is true for content marketing and paid promotions.

In the previous chapters, you learned how to build a solid content marketing funnel. Now, you will learn how to get better results by using paid channels. If you reverse the process — if you spend money to promote your content without fixing your content marketing funnel first — you're building an airplane with no chance of taking off. You're just going to waste your money and time.

So, Why Spend?

You might be thinking...

"Well, if paid promotions are like an enhancer or booster to my overall content marketing, do I really need to spend?"

Here's the reality: there's too much content out there. While great content will help you get the results that you want, it will take longer if you just rely on organic growth and organic channels. Using paid promotions serves as a catalyst for content marketing success, which is especially important if you need to hit time-sensitive business targets.

Also, unless you've been hiding under a rock, you probably know how social media platforms have implemented several changes on how they display content in their feeds. I have heard several businesses complaining how the visibility of their posts have declined dramatically. Even Instagram influencers took a hit.

The reality is this: social media networks are businesses and they need to deliver for their investors.

According to Neil Patel, businesses are only able to reach 6% of their fans without ads. As far as content marketing goes, that is bad. He adds: "It used to be that you could grow a social media following with some creativity and determination. Now, however, you also need dollar bills. And the more you have, the better you'll be able to reach your audience. That is, of course, on purpose. Social media sites want you to pay to reach your ideal market. They don't want you to be able to reach it for free, and they definitely don't want you to be able to go viral without paying for it. Over the years, that truth is only becoming more prevalent. As social media platforms establish themselves, they can require businesses pay more to reach their target markets. And they are doing so. Vehemently."[1]

Why You Shouldn't Be Afraid to Advertise

As a business owner myself, I understand that when it comes to marketing, you want to keep the costs as low as possible. In fact, cost-efficiency is one of the biggest reasons why content marketing has become so popular in the first place.

An "ads-phobic" mentality is a natural knee-jerk reaction.

However, what's really good about online advertising is you don't have to spend thousands of dollars to start. Gone are the days when it would cost you an arm and a leg to run even the most modest ads in traditional media -- TV, radio, and print. With online advertising, you can start for as low as 5 USD per day. You control how much you want to spend and scale from there once you find something that works for you.

Paid online promotions are so cost-efficient that I see many marketers spend on ads to test product concepts and sales messages.

RECOMMENDED STRATEGY

Promoting content through paid channels requires a different approach compared to the more sales-oriented advertising campaigns. Traditional, intrusive, hard sell advertising won't work for content marketing because it defeats the purpose of providing "results in advance" (providing benefits to customers even if they haven't bought anything yet).

As alternatives, the following are the more appropriate channels for content marketing paid promotions:

Native Advertising

As its name suggests, native advertising is a form of advertising that looks more native or natural in an environment where it lives. It appears part of the publication's editorial content instead of an ad. Compared to traditional advertising, which is often perceived as intrusive and salesy, native advertising positions your content as trustworthy, relevant, and useful. Native ads are also less subject to banner blindness and ad blockers.

To benefit from native advertising's traffic-boosting effect, make sure to pick content that matches the sites where you want to promote it.

Likewise, before signing a native advertising agreement, do your due diligence to make sure that the audience who will see your content is going to be complementary to your current audience. The operative term is complementary, not the same. This goes for working with publishers individually, as well as native advertising networks such as Outbrain, Taboola, and Nativo– where your content might show up on several publishers' sites at once.[2]

Influencer Marketing

Influencer marketing is one of the oldest tricks in the bag of PR professionals and has recently gained popularity among content marketers.

Influencers have an established following who are highly receptive to their ideas and recommendations. A number of brands, especially starting ones, are eager to tap into the network of influencers because they have the power to raise awareness fast. Since influencers are trusted, getting your content shared by them creates instant credibility, which would take time to build if you were to do it on your own.

Some influencers would share your content for free, but that would entail building a strong online presence first. If you want to fast track the process, you need to engage them for a paid partnership. Just because your budget is tight doesn't mean that you cannot partner with a top influencer in your field. To lower down the ad rates, you can offer discounted rates for your products and services exclusively for their followers. Also, if you're able to find influencers that share your brand's passion and advocacy, negotiating lower ad rates is more achievable.

Paid Social Media Promotions

On January 11, 2018, Facebook creator Mark Zuckerberg made a big announcement which sent brands scrambling to change how they do Facebook marketing. Here are some excerpts from that announcement:

> *"We built Facebook to help people stay connected and bring us closer together with the people that matter to us. That's why we've always put friends and family at the core of the experience. Research shows that strengthening our relationships improves our well-being and happiness.*
>
> *But recently we've gotten feedback from our community that public content -- posts from businesses, brands and media -- is crowding out the personal moments that lead us to connect more with each other."*
>
> *"Based on this, we're making a major change to how we build Facebook. I'm changing the goal I give our product teams from focusing on helping you*

find relevant content to helping you have more meaningful social interactions."

"As we roll this out, you'll see less public content like posts from businesses, brands, and media. And the public content you see more will be held to the same standard -- it should encourage meaningful interactions between people."

"Now, I want to be clear: by making these changes, I expect the time people spend on Facebook and some measures of engagement will go down. But I also expect the time you do spend on Facebook will be more valuable. And if we do the right thing, I believe that will be good for our community and our business over the long term too.

At its best, Facebook has always been about personal connections. By focusing on bringing people closer together -- whether it's with family and friends, or around important moments in the world -- we can help make sure that Facebook is time well spent."[3]

The roll out did affect the engagement level of organic Facebook posts from brands and business. Plus, it didn't just hit Facebook, it also affected Instagram, which Facebook acquired. Some influencers even reported that the level of engagement they were getting dropped drastically.

Of course, there's still value to creating organic social media content, but it's no longer enough, especially if you're looking to get results fast. You need paid social media promotions to make sure that your content makes it to the newsfeed of your target audience.

Again, the good news is, you can pay to play in social media without breaking the bank. You can start with a modest budget as you are starting out and scale from there once you figure out the best ad content and format that to bring you the best results. Likewise, the big social media platforms including Facebook, Twitter, Instagram, LinkedIn, and Snapchat offer ads in several formats such as videos, image carousels, boosted posts, etc. that benefit content marketers.

Retargeting ads is also an effective way to use paid social media promotions to boost the visibility of your content... in a more strategic/tactical way. Based on people's previous interactions with your brand/business, you can serve or feed them custom ads unique to these past interactions.

Paid Search

Everyday, 3.5 billion Google searches are done, which totals to 1.2 trillion searches every year. The phrase "Google it" is now synonymous with the act of finding information online. Ranking high on Google's SERPs is every content marketer's dream, but it's becoming more difficult as the number of organic links on Google's page one results is decreasing to an average of 8.5 from a previous 10. Also, according to HubSpot's research, 3 out of 4 Google searchers never scroll past the first page of results.[4]

Again, the ultimate goal is to get ranked organically, but this takes time. To be perfectly frank, while some businesses can achieve results from organic rankings, those who are willing to invest in paid promotions to promote their content will always have leverage.

Fortunately, just like social media paid promotions, advertising in search engines doesn't have to be expensive and you have total control over your spending. Analytics are also readily available so you can immediately discontinue paid search campaigns that are not working.

YOU CAN CHOOSE NOT TO "PAY TO PLAY," BUT...

Remember what I said about being prepared to run a marathon if you want to do content marketing? Well, if there are speed boosters in marathons, paid promotions are their equivalent in content marketing. You will still need to follow the process and go through every stage of the content marketing success roadmap. However, paid promotions -- when done right -- can amplify, magnify, and expedite your content marketing success.

RECOMMENDED TOOLS

- Advertising platforms: Facebook,[5] Outbrain,[6] Twitter,[7] Google[8]
- Finding influencers and email: BuzzSumo,[9] Hunter.io[10]
- Facebook Advertising[11] policies and Facebook Ads Guide[12]

SCOPE OF WORK

- Shortlist 5 of your best content that you can promote on Facebook
- Create one ad each for the 5 content pieces and run it on Facebook for one week at $5 a day and monitor the results you're getting (adjust based on your budget)
- Find 10 influencers that are relevant to your niche and pitch your content to them

METRICS TO TRACK

- # of visitors coming from paid channels
- # of leads and sales from paid channels
- # of visitors, engagement, leads, and sales from influencer marketing

CHAPTER 18: THE LEADSPANDA 2X CONTENT MARKETING RESULTS METHOD

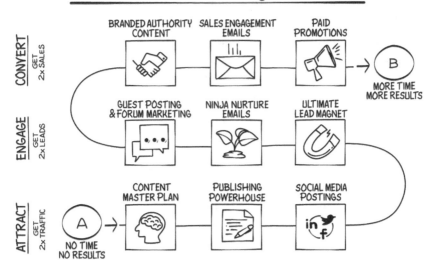

18.1: Proven method that will double your content marketing results in 12 months or less.

Betweeen managing your sales, balancing your books, and other crucial business functions, where do you fit in content marketing?

Consider the following:

- It takes more than 10,000 hours to learn the ins and outs of content marketing and become an expert
- It takes at least 10 hours to put together one high-converting blog post
- Trial and error content marketing can burn thousands of dollars before you figure out something that works
- The hiring process for in-house or freelance writers can take up to 40 hours per hire and 10 hours per week managing them

It comes as no surprise that lack of time is the major obstacle hindering marketers, entrepreneurs, and small business owners from achieving content marketing success. In fact, according to a HubSpot report: "Creating genuinely thought-provoking content is not easy. It's difficult to make and takes more time from concept to completion than many can permit – reducing the competition. Those that put in the extra time and resources will reap the rewards, e.g. coverage on the biggest sites of the highest authority."[1]

Admitting that you don't have the internal capabilities to perform the many tasks and requirements that are crucial to successful content marketing is 100% okay. The more you deny this reality, the farther you will be from achieving the results that you desire.

Remember the story of the two groups of mountain climbers that we talked about at the beginning of this book? Allow me to refresh your memory.

There were two groups of climbers set on reaching the summit of a high-altitude mountain. Both groups started their trek at the same time, but they had different strategies.

Group 1 employed the services of a guide. Since they had an expert on their side, they approached their climb with a clear methodology -- taking things at a slow steady pace, taking strategic breaks in between, and employing other climbing strategies such as breathing techniques to conserve and maximize their energy.

Group 2 went on a DIY route. They were focused on reaching the mountain's summit as fast as possible. There was no structure to their climb.

At the early stages of the trek, Group 2 was ahead of Group 1 as the latter sustained their slow steady pace and took scheduled breaks along the way. However, as the climb continued, the members of Group 2 became exhausted. At some point, they ran out of energy and resources, forcing them to give up.

Trailing at first, Group 1 eventually closed the gap and caught up with Group 2. More important, they were able to reach the summit, which was the ultimate goal of the climb.

What made the difference?

Group 1 possessed 3 primary things that Group 2 did not: expert guidance, the right strategy, and consistency in execution.

3 Ingredients for Content Marketing Success

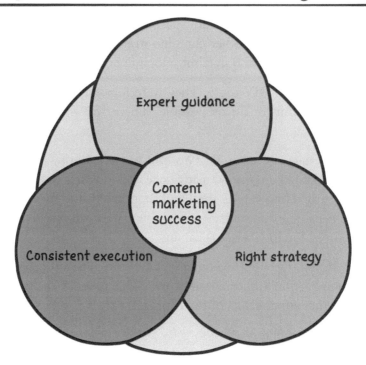

Fig 18.2: 20% of the content marketing activities that generate 80% of the results.

Why did these things matter? These things constitute 20% of the entire climb, but they produced 80% of the results. This is the classic Pareto Principle which states that 20% of the things that you do in life or in business produce 80% of the outcome.

The first step is to recognize that you need a guide, at least while you become a content marketing master of your own. Instead of doing a hundred things that don't produce results, you're better off enlisting the help of a guide that will show you the 20% that really matter.

Partnering with an agency for your content marketing requirements is a good business decision and a worthwhile investment that you can make. If you choose to partner with LeadsPanda, you will benefit from a unique solution called the *2X Content Marketing Results Method* which will give you twice the traffic, twice the leads, and twice the sales you're currently getting in 12 months or less.

Let's go through the different elements of this framework one by one.

ATTRACT - GET 2X TRAFFIC

When there's traffic, there's opportunity. The Attract Stage in the 2X Content Marketing Results Method is aimed at doubling the traffic you're getting.

1. Content Masterplan

Every effective content marketing strategy is built on a solid content masterplan. In order to ensure that you're getting not just traffic, but the right kind of traffic, this stage will include:

- Identifying your target audience/customers (content avatars)
- A survey of your competitors and what they're doing in terms of content marketing
- A comprehensive keyword research to make sure every content you get is optimized for both readers and search engines

The next step involves putting together a list of topics that will be relevant and useful to your customers. The final output is a content calendar that is ready to be implemented in order to help you become a...

2. Publishing Powerhouse

With a solid foundation and a carefully thought out content master-plan, it's the end goal of the Attract Stage to transform you into a publishing powerhouse through the consistent publishing of high-quality content on your own blog.

3. Social Media Postings

Social media marketing is a crucial component in a successful content marketing strategy. If you're not on social media, you are practically invisible. We will create a social media posting calendar for you and craft engaging social media content to drive traffic to your blog and website.

ENGAGE - GET 2X LEADS

Now that you're getting twice (or more) the traffic, it's time to convert them into leads that you can nurture. In the Engage Stage of the 2X Content Marketing Results Method, the 3 main aspects are the following:

4. Ultimate Lead Magnet/s

Results in advance — this is why using lead magnets is a time-tested way to grow an email list. We will come up with lead magnet ideas that will get you the highest possible opt-in rate from the traffic you're getting.

Of course, a great lead magnet is useless if you're unable to "sell" it to your audience. For that, you need a high converting landing page that features compelling copy and design elements. As content and conversion experts, we can help you not only put together an irresistible content magnet offer, but also a landing page that will make it a no-brainer for your audience to give you their emails and download your content.

5. Ninja Nurture Emails

The first few weeks of your new leads in your email list are important. You need to send them strategic, meaningful, and useful content that would allow you to eventually convert leads into paying customers. With the 2X Content Marketing Results Method, we will provide you with a well thought out email nurture sequence so you can engage your new leads effectively.

6. Guest Posting & Forum Marketing

To get more leads, you need to tap previously unexplored sources. We do this by creating a guest posting and forum marketing strategy for your business. Significant research goes into compiling a list of publications and sites that we can pitch for guest blogging. We will do all the heavy lifting — from researching topics, pitching the ideas, to the actual writing of the posts. Regarding forum marketing, we will create a list of relevant questions related to your brand and business. We will search these forums for relevant questions and craft answers on your behalf.

CONVERT - GET 2X SALES

All your content marketing efforts should contribute to the fulfillment of a business goal, and for many businesses including yours, the ultimate objective is to grow revenue. The final stage of the 2X Content Marketing Results Method, Convert, is dedicated to this goal.

7. Branded Authority Content

At this point, you need to shift your relationship with your leads from an information provider to a solutions provider. At this point, we will be putting together content pieces such as whitepapers and case studies that will establish your credibility and authority, while still providing high-quality, valuable content.

8. Sales Engagement Emails

At this stage, all emails sent to your leads should move them into the next stage of the content marketing funnel which is to close the sale. We will craft a sales oriented autoresponder that will pitch your products and services, without the annoying old-school hard sell tactics.

9. Paid Promotions

While organic content marketing tactics and strategies can bring results to your business, it will take longer to achieve business-changing, high-impact results. Combining organic content strategies with paid promotions can give your content marketing significant momentum and accelerate your success.

NO TIME, NO RESULTS –> MORE TIME, MORE RESULTS

Needless to say, planning, executing, and maintaining a successful content marketing strategy is not a walk in the park. It takes time, a lot of brainpower, and a ton of hard work. Small businesses and marketers won't always have the in-house capabilities to do content marketing. As a result, they feel that they lack the time to do content marketing that produces positive results for their business.

Partnering with an agency requires an investment, but the results should give you positive returns. As an example, the LeadsPanda 2X Content Marketing Results Method can help you generate 2X more traffic, 2X more leads, and 2X more sales in 12 months or less.

CHAPTER 19: THE DOS AND DON'TS OF CONTENT MARKETING

T he devil is in the details - so the old adage goes.

Allow us to paraphrase that as it relates to content marketing:

The devil is in the basic details.

Sometimes, content marketers get too fixated on complicated strategies and techniques that fundamentals tend to get ignored, resulting in content marketing campaigns that require maximum effort, but produce minimal results.

This has happened several times in the history of online marketing. Remember the time when businesses got obsessed with fancy flash websites that use really cool animations, but are extremely slow to load and didn't really do anything much for conversions? This is a good example of how marketers can sometimes reinvent the wheel for the sake of "sophistication" instead of sticking to what works for their business and listening to what their customers want.

Back in 2016 as the year drew to a close, Steve Olenski, dubbed as *The CMO Whisperer*, was asked what content marketing prediction he had for 2017. This was his reply: "What I want to see happen in 2017 is that marketers will stop over-complicating and over-thinking essentially everything. It never ceases to amaze me as to the number of consumers who complain they get too much content that is not relevant to them. In today's world that should never happen. What I fear will happen in 2017, however, is that marketers en masse will continue to fiddle with and tinker with essentially everything instead of keeping it simple and giving the people what they want, when they want it, and how they want it."[1]

This is why we decided that it's just fitting to dedicate a section of this e-book to the basics: the dos and don'ts of content marketing. After giving you a content marketing roadmap, we want to take you back to the fundamentals of content marketing to ensure that there's a conscious effort on your end to build a solid foundation for all your content marketing campaigns.

THE DOS

1. Constantly check your content against your customer avatar.

It's easy to lose track of who you're creating content for or fall into the trap of writing for yourself rather than writing for your audience. Constantly revisit your customer avatar and after writing every piece of content, always ask yourself how it would benefit your ideal customer.

Many marketers, including myself, have fallen into the trap of creating self-indulging content. I always have to remind myself and my team: what appeals to us may not always what our audience wants to read. We had several pieces that flopped not because they were badly written, but because they were not resonating with our audience. I know, it can be demoralizing. I mean, if you -- the person who best understands your business and your niche -- would find what you wrote extremely helpful, why would your customers not like it?

Totally understandable reaction. However, at the end of the day, this marketing truth remains: You are not your customer.

2. Always consider platform-content compatibility.

Every platform requires different elements in order for your content to reach your audience effectively. Your Facebook posts cannot be re-posted as is on LinkedIn and vice versa. Take time to customize your content for each channel you use. That said, it doesn't mean that you cannot cross-promote your content across these different platforms. For example, you can promote every blog post you publish on your different social media assets, you just need to tailor fit your social media posts to meet the content expectations on each of them.

3. Track your content via a content calendar.

The content calendar is the Swiss knife of content marketers. Apart from serving as a schedule of when and where your content will be published, it also fulfills several functions such as:

- A collaboration tool where you and your team can contribute content topics/ideas
- An SEO strategy sheet where you can track your target keywords, both short tail, and long tail
- A monitoring sheet where you can track how previously published content performed and which ones can be repurposed

4. Have an editor to polish your content.

While it is true that you might be the most knowledgeable person when it comes to your business, you might not be the most equipped to edit and polish your content. You need a second set of eyes to edit your content, a professional editor that can take a good piece of content to one that fulfills a marketing goal.

5. Measure your content's performance.

When we write content, we do it with a business goal in mind. Not to win a Pulitzer prize or to look cool or because everyone else is doing it. Content marketing is all about driving business results. Otherwise, your content marketing is just like deceptive appearances -- All that glitters is not gold!

Measuring your content marketing's ROI is a must. This is because over the course of doing it, you will have several hits and misses. You need to have the ability to tell definitively, using empirical data, which tactics produced positive business results and which ones are flops. This will allow you to iterate from the strategies that delivered positive business impact.

THE DON'TS

1. Make content you like.

It's human nature to see things from our own perspectives. However, unless YOU are your business' ideal customer, avoid using what you like and what you do as the baseline for developing your content. Instead, ask questions to your target audience to find out what they want. Do your homework about the different content platforms out there and who they reach, and put the right content in front of the right people.

A top myth about content is that it's about your company or you. Make sure it appeals to your current target audience. Write content that will help them, address their needs, and improve their lives.

2. Expect to set it and forget it.

Content is constant. Unlike the print ads and billboards of yesteryear, you can't set up your campaign and let it run untouched for weeks or even hours at a time. Consistent, real-time engagement is critical in kickstarting the brand conversation in your space. Being mindful of the relevancy and timing of your content will lead to gains in user interactions and brand engagement. 50% of content marketers surveyed in a 2015 B2B content marketing trends study say that producing content consistently is a major challenge.[2]

3. Mute your audience.

Muting your audience is one of the worst things you can do for your content strategy. Businesses have an inherent – and justified – fear of the all-powerful negative review, the enraged blog comment, and the nasty rebuttal retweet. But have no fear; letting your current and potential consumers speak their minds is a healthy and sometimes even helpful way to address their concerns and make your business better. According to a survey by Bazaarvoice, 7 out of 10 negative reviewers said their opinion was changed after receiving a response, and it helped positively shape the opinion of potential buyers seeing the dialogue.[3]

4. Be a robot.

People see right through businesses churning out content just to do it, especially if it holds no value. If you're not going to do your content right, it's better to not do it at all. Content marketing is the opportunity to build your brand message in a truly organic and honest way; let your audience know you, connect with you, and learn from you. According to a study by the Content Marketing Institute and MarketingProfs, 54% of content marketers say that producing engaging content is their biggest challenge.[4]

5. Do it alone if you don't have the in-house resources.

Content marketing is very hands-on, and it's challenging for businesses to do it all themselves. Working with experienced marketers who can make the most of your investment, create content that is effective, and maintain a consistent presence on key digital platforms is a good way to succeed in content marketing. Look for a strategic partner that will take the time to get to know your business and understand your voice, so your content is not only authentic, but also drives results. Roughly 62% of businesses today are outsourcing their content marketing.[5]

NOW TAKE ACTION!

Now that you have the information and the tools; now that you have an overview of how things work and how to leverage on strategic content marketing—what are your next steps?

Set aside time so you can put all your new skills to good use.

It's not quite as overwhelming as you think it is. Each chapter of this book serves as a guide that lets you take actionable steps towards a strategic and effective content marketing plan. Keep in mind that this is a tried and tested process—the same one that we ourselves have implemented to grow our business.

Because no two businesses are exactly alike, you can, of course, expect some differences in the results. Regardless of what factors contribute to the varying outcomes, know that these are your first steps towards a more comprehensive and effective content marketing effort. It's a learning process; and along the way, rest assured that you will learn and tweak your approach so that you are able to execute a strategy that is optimized for your own unique business needs.

Avoid taking shortcuts and don't rush through the process. As with anything in life, the more effort you invest into something, the more benefits you reap from it. You've already put in the time and effort to learn about how you can do content marketing right…don't stop now. Trust me, it's well worth the effort.

This reminds me of a story, a parable, that one of my teachers from school told us about.

A terrible storm is about to hit a small town so the mayor sent out a warning to everyone and encouraged residents to evacuate and find a safe place to stay in while waiting for the storm to pass.

A religious man prayed to God to keep him safe and he had a vision of God extending his hand to lead him to safe grounds.

The storm arrived and the town started flooding. Some of the man's neighbors came by his house and asked if he would like to come with them as they still had room in their pickup truck. The man said no.

The strong rain continued and it soon flooded the man's living room so he had to retreat to the second floor. A few minutes after, a motorboat came by with rescuers. They urged him to come with them, but he said no.

The man kept on praying and the rain continued to pour violently. It didn't take long for the floodwater to reach the second floor where the man was staying. He was forced to climb to the roof. He continued to pray.

A few minutes after, a helicopter flew by and the rescuers threw a ladder to the man so he could be rescued. The man refused, still believing that his vision would come true.

The rain didn't stop. Without any higher ground to seek refuge in, the man drowned and died.

In heaven, the man asked God why he had forsaken him.

God replied: "Your mayor gave out a warning. I sent you a truck, a motorboat, and a helicopter. What more were you looking for?"

The morale of the story: Act Now. You have all the information you need to run a successful content marketing program.

Everything you just read in this book are all the content marketing lifelines that you need. Sure, there's a wealth of content marketing knowledge out there that's not mentioned in this book, but everything you need to take action and get the ball rolling you just read. Don't wait. Don't procrastinate. Your competitors aren't.

Roll your sleeves up and get to work. And remember, if you need guidance, I and the entire LeadsPanda team are ready to help.

Sincerely,

Prafull Sharma

PS. If you want to start a conversation about this topic, ask a question, want to clarify something, even if you simply just want to say hi, please send me an email at cmb@leadspanda.com. I regularly check that email and rest assured, you will hear back from me.

THANK YOU FOR READING MY BOOK

Thanks a ton.

I hope it helps you to become a better content marketer.

Drop a line to cmb@leadspanda.com and let me know how it's going. I really appreciate all of your feedback, and I love hearing what you have to say.

Your input will make the next version better.

Please remember to leave me a helpful REVIEW at your favorite retailer.

Thanks so much!!!

~ Prafull

NOTES

Introduction

1. Content Marketing Institute,
   https://contentmarketinginstitute.com/wp-content/uploads/2015/04/2015_Enterprise_Research_FINAL.pdf
2. History Channel, "D-Day",
   https://www.history.com/topics/world-war-ii/d-day

Chapter 1

1. Content Marketing Institute, "What is Content Marketing", https://contentmarketinginstitute.com/what-is-content-marketing/
2. Copyblogger, Demian Farnworth, "What Is Content Marketing?", https://www.copyblogger.com/content-marketing-codex/
3. Page Fair, "The 2015 Ad Blocking Report", https://pagefair.com/blog/2015/ad-blocking-report/
4. Marketing Land, Anthony Muller, "Ad-mageddon! Ad

blocking, its impact, and what comes next",
https://marketingland.com/ad-mageddon-perspectives-ad-blocking-impacts-comes-next-227090

5. Cloud Living, Doug Beney, "EBook Launch Case Study: How Doug Made $3000 In 2 Weeks With An Email List Of Just 2,500", https://www.cloudliving.com/ebook-launch-success/

6. Kapost, Christine Leas, "8 More Content Marketing Stats to Knock Your Socks (Back)", https://kapost.com/b/content-marketing-stats/

7. Alexa, http://searchenginejournal.com Competitive Analysis, Marketing Mix and Traffic, https://www.alexa.com/siteinfo/searchenginejournal.com

8. Medium, Shane Barker, "Case Study: How I Grew My Website Traffic from 50K to 90K in 6 Months", https://medium.com/swlh/case-study-how-i-grew-my-website-traffic-from-50k-to-90k-in-6-months-3edfde923234

9. Demand Metric, Content Marketing Infographic, https://www.demandmetric.com/content/content-marketing-infographic

10. Aberdeen, "Crossing the Chaos: Managing Content Marketing Transformation", http://resources.kapost.com/rs/kapoststd/images/Aberdeen_Managing_Content_Marketing_Transformation.pdf

11. Digital Vidya, Ritu Jhajharia, "Content Marketing Case Studies: 5 Brands Demonstrate How it's done!", https://www.digitalvidya.com/blog/content-marketing-case-studies/

Chapter 2

1. Content Marketing Institute, Jodi Harris, "How to Develop a Content Strategy: Start With These 3 Questions", https://contentmarketinginstitute.com/2019/09/questions-content-strategy/

2. Buffer, https://buffer.com/

3. The Fletcher Method,
   https://go.fletchermethod.com/hp-1

Chapter 3

1. Marketing Land, Daniel Faggella, "How to optimize your content for each step of the buyer's journey",
   https://marketingland.com/optimize-content-step-buyers-journey-162239
2. Neil Patel, "When Can You Expect Your Content Marketing Efforts to Bear Fruit?",
   https://neilpatel.com/blog/when-can-you-expect-your-content-marketing-efforts-to-bear-fruit/
3. Entrepreneur, Karl Naim, "Why Content Marketing Needs To Be At The Heart Of Your Customer Acquisition Strategy", https://www.entrepreneur.com/article/310725
4. Teachable, Eduardo Yi, "How to Build a Marketing Funnel That Generates Massive Sales",
   https://teachable.com/blog/marketing-funnel

Chapter 4

1. Buffer, Adrath Albee via Kevan Lee, "The Complete, Actionable Guide to Marketing Personas",
   https://buffer.com/library/marketing-personas-beginners-guide
2. Forbes, Jason Demers, "6 Steps to Decoding Your Target Audience",
   https://www.forbes.com/sites/jaysondemers/%202013/08/27/6-steps-to-decoding-your-target-audience/
3. Mind Control, Frank Kern,
   https://frankkern.com/frankkern/customerhub/mindcontrol/mindcontrol.pdf
4. Claritas, My Best Segments, https://claritas360.claritas.com/mybestsegments/

5. Qualaroo, https://qualaroo.com/
6. Survey Monkey, https://www.surveymonkey.com/
7. Think With Google, https://www.thinkwithgoogle.com/

Chapter 5

1. Search Engine Watch, Rob D. Young, " Who Uses Search Engines? 92% of Adult U.S. Internet Users", https://www.searchenginewatch.com/2011/08/11/who-uses-search-engines-92-of-adult-u-s-internet-users-study/
2. Moz, "The Beginner's Guide to SEO", https://moz.com/beginners-guide-to-seo/keyword-research
3. Search Engine Land, Janet Driscoll Miller, "Mapping keywords to the buyer journey in SEO", https://searchengineland.com/mapping-keywords-buyer-journey-seo-270862
4. IntuitSolutions, "Case Study: Competitor Keyword Analysis & Content Strategy Process", https://www.intuitsolutions.net/case-study-competitor-keyword-analysis-content-strategy-hairbow-company/
5. Google Keyword Planner, https://ads.google.com/intl/en_ph/home/tools/keyword-planner/
6. Neil Patel, Ubersuggest, https://neilpatel.com/ubersuggest/
7. WordStream, https://www.wordstream.com/keywords

Chapter 6

1. Marketing Sherpa, "Social Media Marketing: AT&T Developer Program calendar strategy increases Twitter audience 136%, Facebook 113%", https://www.marketingsherpa.com/article/case-study/att-developer-program-content-calendar
2. Buzzsumo, https://buzzsumo.com/

3. Wordpress, Editorial Calendar Plugin, https://wordpress.org/plugins/editorial-calendar/

Chapter 7

1. Entrepreneur, Mike Kappel, "Why Your Small Business Must Start a Blog", https://www.entrepreneur.com/article/271049
2. Hubspot, Rick Burnes, "Study Shows Business Blogging Leads to 55% More Website Visitors", https://blog.hubspot.com/blog/tabid/6307/bid/5014/study-shows-business-blogging-leads-to-55-more-website-visitors.aspx
3. Hubspot, "Lead Generation Tips From 1400 Websites", https://web.archive.org/web/20120718045235/http://www.hubspot.com/lead-generation-tips/
4. Hubspot, "Lead Generation Tips From 1400 Websites", https://web.archive.org/web/20120718045235/http://www.hubspot.com/lead-generation-tips/
5. Pagezii, "How to Increase Lead Generation by +250% with your Blog", https://blog.pagezii.com/lead-generation-blogging/
6. CoSchedule's Headline Analyzer, https://coschedule.com/headline-analyzer
7. SEMrush.com, https://www.semrush.com/
8. Google Keyword Planner, https://ads.google.com/intl/en_in/home/tools/keyword-planner/
9. Readable, https://readable.io/
10. Canva, https://www.canva.com/
11. Copyscape, https://www.copyscape.com/
12. ConversionMonk, http://conversionmonk.com/
13. Google Analytics, https://analytics.google.com/analytics/web/

Chapter 8

1. Buffer, Kevan Lee, "We Stopped Publishing New Blog Posts for One Month. Here's What Happened.", https://buffer.com/resources/blog-strategies
2. Alexa, http://slideshare.net Competitive Analysis, Marketing Mix and Traffic, https://www.alexa.com/siteinfo/slideshare.net
3. Hubspot, Clifford Chi, "51 YouTube Stats Every Video Marketer Should Know in 2019", https://blog.hubspot.com/marketing/youtube-stats
4. Edison Research, "The Infinite Dial 2018 Report", https://www.edisonresearch.com/infinite-dial-2018/
5. Canva, https://www.canva.com/
6. Piktochart, https://piktochart.com/
7. Google Slides, https://www.google.com/slides/about/
8. Slide Share, https://www.slideshare.net/
9. Scribd, https://www.scribd.com/
10. Camtasia, https://www.techsmith.com/video-editor.html
11. ScreenFlow, https://www.telestream.net/screenflow/overview.htm
12. YouTube, https://www.youtube.com/
13. Libsyn, https://libsyn.com/
14. Buzzsprout, https://www.buzzsprout.com/

Chapter 9

1. Impact, Tom DiScipio, "How to Create a Lead Magnet (& 9 Awesome Examples to Inspire Yours)", https://www.impactbnd.com/blog/how-to-create-a-lead-magnet
2. Dr. Dan Ariely, "Predictably Irrational, Revised and Expanded Edition: The Hidden Forces That Shape Our Decisions", https://www.goodreads.com/book/show/6554875-predictably-irrational
3. Hubspot Landing Page Tool, https://offers.hubspot.com/free-trial-landing-pages

4. Leadpages, https://www.leadpages.net/
5. Unbounce, https://unbounce.com/

Chapter 10

1. Hubspot, Peter Gracey, "98% of Your MQLs Will Never Result in Closed Business", https://blog.hubspot.com/sales/98-of-your-mqls-will-never-result-in-closed-business
2. Hubspot, Doug Davidoff, "The Executive's Guide to Effective Lead Nurturing Programs", https://blog.hubspot.com/marketing/executive-guide-effective-lead-nurturing
3. DemandGen Report, "Calculating The Real ROI From Lead Nurturing", https://www.demandgenreport.com/industry-resources/white-papers/204-calculating-the-real-roi-from-lead-nurturing-.html
4. Annuitas, "Let's Ease Into It", https://www.annuitas.com/blog/2010/03/29/lets-ease-into-it/
5. Aberdeen, "Event Marketing: Best-in-class Companies Integrate Events With Multi-channel Marketing Strategy", http://www.aberdeen.com/research/8740/ra-event-lead-marketing/content.aspx
6. Marketing Sherpa, "Lead Nurturing: Pilot campaign increases conversion 32.6% with automated", https://www.marketingsherpa.com/article/case-study/pilot-campaign-increases-conversion-326
7. Crazy Egg, "How to Turn Your SaaS Lead Nurturing Efforts into Lead Optimization Wins", https://www.crazyegg.com/blog/lead-optimization-wins/
8. Mailchimp, https://mailchimp.com/
9. AWeber, https://www.aweber.com/
10. Infusionsoft, https://keap.com/infusionsoft

Chapter 11

1. Donald Miller, "Building a StoryBrand: Clarify Your Message So Customers Will Listen Hardcover – October 10, 2017", https://www.goodreads.com/book/show/34460583-building-a-storybrand
2. Camtasia, https://www.techsmith.com/video-editor.html
3. Screenflow, http://www.telestream.net/screenflow/overview.htm
4. Hubspot Landing Page Tool, https://offers.hubspot.com/free-trial-landing-pages
5. Leadpages, https://www.leadpages.net/
6. Unbounce, https://unbounce.com/

Chapter 12

1. eMarketer, "Email Outperforms Social Media, Paid Search for ROI", https://www.emarketer.com/Article/Email-Outperforms-Social-Media-Paid-Search-ROI/1014905
2. Unbounce, Jessica Moon, "Creating Irresistible Email Teaser Campaigns [Case Study]", https://unbounce.com/email-marketing/email-teaser-campaign/
3. OpenView, "Research Finds Email Driving More Consumers to Purchase Than Facebook, Text Messaging Combined", https://openviewpartners.com/research-finds-email-driving-more-consumers-to-purchase-than-facebook-text-messaging-combined/#.XekF_pIzbVo
4. Mailchimp, https://mailchimp.com/
5. AWeber, https://www.aweber.com/
6. Infusionsoft by Keap, https://keap.com/infusionsoft

Chapter 13

1. Quick Sprout, "12 Tips to Increase Webinar Conversions", https://www.quicksprout.com/webinar-conversions/
2. Digital Course Academy, Amy Porterfield, http://www.amyporterfield.com/webinarsthatconvert/
3. Rob Falcone, "Just F*ing Demo!: Tactics for Leading Kickass Product Demos", https://www.goodreads.com/book/show/23571774-just-f-ing-demo
4. WebinarJam, https://www.webinarjam.com/
5. Go To Webinar, https://www.gotomeeting.com/webinar
6. Uberconference, https://www.uberconference.com/
7. Go To Meeting, https://www.gotomeeting.com/
8. Skype, https://www.skype.com/en/

Chapter 14

1. Gary Vaynerchuk, "Jab, Jab, Jab, Right Hook: How to Tell Your Story in a Noisy Social World", https://www.goodreads.com/book/show/17383989-jab-jab-jab-right-hook
2. GlobalWebIndex, Katie Young, "Social Media Captures Over 30% of Online Time", https://blog.globalwebindex.com/chart-of-the-day/social-media-captures-30-of-online-time/
3. We Are Social, Simon Kemp, "Digital In 2018: World's Internet Users Pass The 4 Billion Mark", https://wearesocial.com/blog/2018/01/global-digital-report-2018
4. Coschedule, Ben Sailer, "The Best Times to Post on Social Media in 2019 According to 25 Studies", https://coschedule.com/blog/best-times-to-post-on-social-media/
5. Hubspot, Daria Marmer, "How Frequently Should I Publish on Social Media? A HubSpot Experiment", https://blog.hubspot.com/marketing/how-frequently-should-i-publish-on-social-media

6. Digital Training Academy, "Whiskas creates Kitten Kollege on YouTube", http://www.digitaltrainingacademy.com/casestudies/2017 /09/whiskas_creates_kitten_kollege_on_youtube.php
7. Neilsen, "Under The Influence: Consumer Trust In Advertising", https://www.nielsen.com/us/en/insights/article/2013/un der-the-influence-consumer-trust-in-advertising/
8. Buffer, https://buffer.com/
9. Hootsuite, https://hootsuite.com/
10. Meet Edgar, https://meetedgar.com/

Chapter 15

1. Search Engine Watch, Eric Siu, "How Guest Posting Propelled One Site From 0 to 100,000 Customers", https://www.searchenginewatch.com/2012/07/26/how-guest-posting-propelled-one-site-from-0-to-100000-customers/
2. Gregory Ciotti, "Guest blogging strategies that helped grow 36,733 email subscribers", https://www.gregoryciotti.com/guest-blogging/
3. Neil Patel, "Why Guest Blogging is The Best Inbound Marketing Strategy (A Data Driven Answer)", https://neilpatel.com/blog/why-guest-blogging-is-the-best-inbound-marketing-strategy-a-data-driven-answer/
4. Growth Tools, Bryan Harris, "3 Lessons I Learned From My First Guest Post (And All My Traffic Numbers)", https://videofruit.com/blog/5-lessons-learned-first-guest-post-traffic-numbers/
5. Hubspot, Clifford Chi, "What Is Domain Authority and How Can You Improve It?", https://blog.hubspot.com/marketing/domain-authority
6. Optimize Smart, "10000 Search Engine Queries for Your Link Building Campaign",

https://www.optimizesmart.com/10000-search-engine-queries-for-your-link-building-campaign/#a23

7. Authority Hacker, Perrin Carrell, "17 Guest Posting Tips I Learned From Failing Thousands Of Times", https://www.authorityhacker.com/guest-posting-tips/

8. Moz, https://moz.com/help/link-explorer

9. Ahrefs, https://ahrefs.com/

Chapter 16

1. Lead Generation Insights, Tim Ohlrich, "How Can You Use Forums To Boost Your Content Marketing Efforts?", https://www.straightnorth.com/insights/how-can-you-use-forums-boost-your-content-marketing-efforts/

2. Pew Internet, "Demographics of Online Discussion Forums", https://www.pewresearch.org/internet/2015/08/19/mobile-messaging-and-social-media-2015/2015-08-19_social-media-update_04/

3. Expanded Ramblings, "12 Interesting Quora Statistics", https://expandedramblings.com/index.php/quora-statistics/

4. The Next Web, Simon Kemp, "Reddit now has more active users than Twitter — and is more engaging than porn", https://thenextweb.com/contributors/2018/04/19/reddit-now-active-users-twitter-engaging-porn/

5. Marketing Conference Service, https://marketing.conference-services.net/resources/327/3554/pdf/AM2013_0198_paper.pdf

6. Forbes, Jules Schroeder, "The Magic Formula Behind Going Viral On Reddit", https://www.forbes.com/sites/julesschroeder/2016/03/10/the-magic-formula-behind-going-viral-on-reddit/

7. Quora, https://www.quora.com/

8. Reddit, https://www.reddit.com/

Chapter 17

1. Neil Patel, "Why Social Media is 'Pay to Play' in 2018 (And How to Get the Best Bang for Your Buck)", https://neilpatel.com/blog/pay-to-play-social-media/
2. Entrepreneur, Cynthia Johnson, "Top 8 Native Advertising Platforms for Advertisers and Publishers", https://www.entrepreneur.com/article/289976
3. Facebook, Mark Zuckerberg, https://www.facebook.com/zuck/posts/10104413015393571
4. Hubspot, Mike Lieberman, "10 Stats About Inbound Marketing That Will Make Your Jaw Drop", https://blog.hubspot.com/insiders/inbound-marketing-stats
5. Facebook, https://www.facebook.com/
6. Outbrain, https://www.outbrain.com/
7. Twitter, https://ads.twitter.com/login
8. Google, https://ads.google.com/intl/en_in/home/
9. Buzzsumo, https://buzzsumo.com/
10. Hunter, https://hunter.io/
11. Facebook Advertising, https://www.facebook.com/policies/ads/
12. Facebook Ads Guide, https://www.facebook.com/business/ads-guide/video

Chapter 18

1. Hubspot, "Driving Content Marketing Success in Europe", http://cdn2.hubspot.net/hubfs/53/Driving_Content_Marketing_2015.pdf

Chapter 19

1. Forbes, Steve Olenski, "Marketers Should Stop

Overcomplicating Everything",
https://www.forbes.com/sites/steveolenski/2017/05/02/
marketers-should-stop-over-complicating-everything

2. Content Marketing Institute, "2015 Benchmarks, Budgets,
    and Trends— North America",
    https://contentmarketinginstitute.com/wp-
    content/uploads/2014/10/2015_B2B_Research.pdf

3. Bazaar Voice, "The Conversation Index Volume 6",
    http://media2.bazaarvoice.com/documents/Bazaarvoice_
    Conversation_Index_Volume6.pdf

4. Content Marketing Institute, "2015 Benchmarks, Budgets,
    and Trends— North America",
    https://contentmarketinginstitute.com/wp-
    content/uploads/2014/10/2015_B2B_Research.pdf

5. Content Marketing Institute, "2012 B2B Content
    Marketing Benchmarks, Budgets and Trends",
    https://contentmarketinginstitute.com/wp-
    content/uploads/2011/12/B2B_Content_Marketing_201
    2.pdf

ABOUT THE AUTHOR

Prafull Sharma is an entrepreneur, marketer, and founder of Leads-Panda. He has successfully launched and grown businesses in the marketing and technology industries. His work has appeared in TechCrunch, Social Media Examiner, Business Insider, and Economic Times. Over the past 8 years, he has helped hundreds of businesses achieve their marketing goals, and double their marketing results; from well-funded startups to leading technology companies, and large enterprises.

leadspanda.com
#CMB

 twitter.com/prafullsha

Made in United States
Troutdale, OR
11/26/2023